"This book is a treasure—nourishing, sustaining, and skillfully crafted. Calling their approach to the release from anxiety 'the way of awareness,' the authors have shaped a warm, authentic rendering of mindfulness practice into direct, easily understandable language. Step by step, they lead us into substantive, well-documented methods for becoming intimately familiar with an inner terrain and integrating what is discovered in this interior realm into a way of being that is the key to freeing us from the imprisoning tyranny of anxiety and fear."

—Saki F. Santorelli, Ed.D., executive director of the Center for Mindfulness in Medicine, Health Care, and Society and associate professor of medicine at the University of Massachusetts Medical School and author of Heal Thyself

daily meditations for calming your anxious mind

JEFFREY BRANTLEY, MD
WENDY MILLSTINE, NC

New Harbinger Publications, Inc.

Distributed in Canada by Raincoast Books

Copyright © 2008 by Jeffrey Brantley and Wendy Millstine
New Harbinger Publications, Inc.
5674 Shattuck Avenue
Oakland, CA 94609
www.newharbinger.com

Cover design by Amy Shoup; Text design by Amy Shoup and Michele Waters-Kermes; Acquired by Tesilya Hanauer; Edited by Elisabeth Beller

Library of Congress Cataloging-in-Publication Data

Brantley, Jeffrey.
  Daily meditations for calming your anxious mind / Jeffrey Brantley, and Wendy Millstine.
    p. cm.
  Includes bibliographical references.
  ISBN-13: 978-1-57224-540-2 (pbk. : alk. paper)
  ISBN-10: 1-57224-540-9 (pbk. : alk. paper) 1. Anxiety. 2. Meditation. I. Matik, Wendy-O, 1966- II. Title.
  BF575.A6B738 2008
  158.1'28--dc22
                        2008003621

14   13   12

10   9   8   7   6

For my friends, whose ceaseless compassion and understanding have been the kindling to the fires of love and inspiration throughout my life.

For my bubi Kayla Sussell, whose blazing spirit of love and guidance has enriched my life beyond my wildest dreams.

—WM

For all who work for peace, justice, and human dignity—may you be protected, and guided by wisdom and compassion.

—JB

Contents

SECTION 2

daily meditations for embracing joys and fears 75

introduction

We live in the present moment.

Our inner life and the outer world meet here and now. Each world interacts, reacts, responds, and to some extent, shapes the other.

Right now, in this moment, what is your relationship to the ever-changing flow of inner and outer life? How much of the process are you aware of? How steady is your attention to the flow? Is your heart filled with curiosity and affection or with dullness, fear, or even dislike for what is with you now? It is these unconscious and habitual inner reactions of body and mind to the real and imagined threats of living that create a prison here, in the present moment.

Meditation is an activity that involves sensitive attention; inclusive, nonjudging awareness; is sustained by attitudes of kindness and compassion; and offers the possibility of deep and wise understanding of yourself and how to live with more ease and happiness. Meditation is also an ancient and diverse inner technology—involving a vast array of different practices——for examining and transforming your inner life and its interaction with the outer world.

Fear is the reaction of mind and body to the presence of a threat or danger. The capacity to react to threat is wired into us, mediated by the sympathetic division of the autonomic nervous system. The incredible cascade of mind-body events that makes up the reaction to threat can also be called the *fight-or-flight response* or *stress response*. Interestingly, the body can be activated to produce the fight-or-flight response when it senses threat or danger outside of itself, as when you hear a siren or smell smoke; or the body can activate the fear response from signals produced by the brain that suggest danger is present, as when you have the thought "I am stuck in traffic, and my whole day is ruined."

Anxiety is the feeling of fear that is out of proportion to the situation or that arises when there is no clear threat or danger in the situation. *Worry* is the mind's manifestation of anxiety, characterized by endless frightened and frightening thoughts about the situation in mind. Inner manifestations of anxiety and worry such as fear of the future or the unknown, fear of taking risks, and self-criticism are examples of a simple principle:

> *Anxiety, excessive fear, and worry arise because you turn away from the present moment and become lost in memories, stories, and beliefs about the past or future.*

The feelings of anxiety and worry themselves are actually part of the present-moment experience and can be seen as such instead of as an absolute truth or an immutable personal defect. The shifting of attention away from the present to someplace else is usually just an unconscious habit of mind—a pattern of paying attention—that you have learned as a means of meeting life's challenges. Unfortunately, such unconscious attention shifts do not often help with feelings of anxiety and upset, but instead lead to increased and repeating distress.

Feelings of separation and isolation arise from inattention to inner reactions and from habitual, defensive patterns expressed through heart, mind, and body. These inner reactions can interrupt your sense of connection to others, drive you to withdraw from and resist the constantly changing conditions in each moment, and imprison you in feelings and stories based on fear and worry.

Yet freedom is closer and more natural than you might think. Peace, ease, joy, and discovery at the wonder and mystery of life are also here, in the present moment. They wait for your presence and attention, living in both your inner and outer worlds, where life itself is constantly unfolding.

THE HEALING POWER OF MINDFULNESS AND COMPASSION

In the companion book to this one, *Calming Your Anxious Mind: How Mindfulness and Compassion Can Free You from Anxiety, Fear, and Panic* (Brantley 2007), the central message is that human beings have within themselves enormous power and potential to radically change the way they experience and interact with life itself, both inner and outer. That includes how they manage the powerful and disturbing energies of anxiety, fear, and panic.

Anxiety and fear will continue their reign over you until you develop the language and skills of inner awareness that empower a different relationship to those energies and to your own habitual reactions to them. The key to accessing your inner power for a different awareness, and the resulting transformation, lies in your ability and commitment to develop *mindfulness*. Mindfulness is an awareness that follows from kind and nonjudging allowing, and from present-moment, centered attention.

> *Just that—learn to stay present, to keep your heart and mind open, and stop trying to change anything; just pay close attention. What happens when you pay attention changes everything.*

Mindful attention in the present moment reveals that anxiety, fear, and panic (and other distressing conditions) are truly temporary and not "you"! A mindful observer realizes further that his or her own reactions to these changing, unpleasant energies are crucial. Habitual, unconscious reactions can perpetuate or make worse the experience of distress and helplessness you feel in their presence—and when those reactions become conscious, they can be replaced by wise responses. Wise responses, in turn, can then reveal enormous freedom and unsuspected richness and possibility in each moment and situation. As you practice mindfulness through various meditations and activities, you may be surprised to experience for yourself how truly vast, beautiful, and alive you already are.

This book, *Daily Meditations for Calming Your Anxious Mind*, is a companion text to *Calming Your Anxious Mind* and a direct response to requests for more meditations and practices based in mindfulness, kindness, and compassion. In these pages you will find meditations, visualizations, affirmations, and thoughtful reflections that anyone can use to meet the challenges of fear, worry, and anxiety in modern life, and to live with more ease and joy.

Mindful attention, with its openhearted and compassionate attitude toward all experience, empowers you to grow awareness and take better care of your inner life and to recognize and nurture a wiser, more effective relationship to your outer world and those in it.

ANYONE CAN MEDITATE, ANYONE CAN BENEFIT

The idea of approaching anxiety, fear, and panic using mindfulness and meditation is based on an evidence-based model for using mindfulness in health and healing known as *mindfulness-based stress reduction* (MBSR). That model was developed by Jon Kabat-Zinn and his colleagues at the University of Massachusetts Medical Center in Worcester, Massachusetts.

Since its beginnings in 1979, the MBSR approach has been shown to offer benefits for treating a variety of medical and psychological conditions, including those marked by anxiety and depression. Literally thousands of individuals worldwide have benefited from this mindfulness-based model, and medical research has confirmed the positive impact that practicing mindfulness can have on many illnesses and conditions.

Because the approach is based in a health care model, these mindfulness-based meditations and practices are available for anyone. Mindfulness meditation does not demand any specific religious or spiritual orientation in the approach presented here to health, healing, and personal transformation. So anyone can practice and benefit from being more mindful!

Neither this book nor its companion book are meant to be self-contained or comprehensive MBSR programs. However, they are both inspired and informed—in philosophy and practices—by the MBSR approach in its application of mindfulness, kindness, and compassion toward anxiety, fear, and panic.

LEARNING TO PRACTICE "BEING, NOT DOING"

All of the practices that you will meet in this book are based, either explicitly or implicitly, on *mindfulness.* Mindfulness is an awareness that is sensitive, open, kind, gentle, and curious. Mindfulness is a basic human capacity. It arises from paying attention on purpose in a way that is nonjudging, friendly, and does not try to add or subtract anything from whatever is happening. This allowing aspect has been called by some *radical acceptance* because it is so radically different from the usual way of relating to experience.

Usually, we try simply to get more of the pleasant things and to get rid of the unpleasant ones. Most of our life energy and, indeed, entire cultures and civilizations, can be driven by this core orientation toward greed for feeling good and hatred for feeling bad.

Being mindful means taking another position. That position is one of gentle, curious, and nonjudging attention, no matter how pleasant or unpleasant the experience is.

It is often said that in practicing mindfulness, you practice *being, not doing.* This means that by practicing mindfulness, you stop trying to change things and start opening, allowing, and noticing what is happening more closely and carefully.

By being willing to notice and radically accept what is present in your inner and outer worlds in this moment (*being*), you give yourself the possibility of freedom from unconscious habits of greed and hatred, which drive the painful and ineffective grasping or fighting of different experiences like anxiety and fear, moment by moment (*doing*).

Being, not doing, then creates the situation where *being informs doing.* That is, by paying attention more closely and connecting more deeply and consciously with the present moment, you are able to stop reacting and to recognize and choose the wisest and most effective responses to any situation life presents.

And if you feel that you don't understand this description of mindfulness, don't worry. You will have plenty of instruction in these pages and meditations ahead. As you practice the meditations, you will probably also realize that you have already been more mindful during your life than you knew! You just didn't call it that.

USING THIS BOOK MOST EFFECTIVELY

In the four main numbered sections of this book, you will find meditations and practices grounded in mindfulness and organized around four core themes:

1.   Relaxing and feeling safe

2.   Embracing joys and fears

3.   Befriending your anxious mind and body

4.   Connecting to the web of life

In the various meditations and practices in these four numbered sections, you will find ways to learn and master the language and skills of inner awareness. These skills will lead to greater understanding of exactly how your inner and outer worlds interact, influence, and interpenetrate each other, moment by moment.

With each new lesson and skill you acquire, you will probably find that life's challenges, including fear and anxiety, lose some of their control over you. You may also be delighted to discover that life's blessings are increasingly visible and available.

Each major theme in this book is simply a point of emphasis for the meditations in that section. In fact, you will probably notice that in a curious, holographic way, the themes—feelings of ease and safety, embracing all experience with mindful attention, relating to anxious experience with kindness and friendliness, and recognition of larger patterns of interconnectedness—emerge repeatedly in different ways throughout all the meditations in this book.

There is, therefore, no "right" way to use this book and no specific order in which to do the meditations. Which meditations you choose and when you practice may vary, literally, day to day and week by week.

The first and most important step is to give yourself time and support to do some meditation every day. What to do next then becomes a journey of discovery and self-care.

We invite you to approach the themes and the various meditations as your friends and allies, getting to know them in your own time and at your own speed. Work with the ones that resonate for you. Learn to trust yourself to know which theme is most needed in your life when, and which meditations offer you the most support and wisdom.

Additionally, in the next section, The Foundation, you will get more information about these themes and their interactions and about using this book, and detailed instructions for practicing mindfulness, kindness, and compassion as meditations.

THE WAY OF AWARENESS

Someone once observed that you cannot stop the waves of life, but you can learn to surf!

Learning to surf the waves of life doesn't happen by accident. When intense energies like anxiety, fear, and panic appear (as well as other challenges such as chronic pain, illness, or disturbing events and conditions in the outer world), your commitment to and experience practicing mindfulness, kindness, and compassion will be needed, and that same experience will support you.

Practicing mindfulness means making the commitment to working with your life, inner and outer, in a radical and amazing way. You are entering the "way" of awareness.

The *way of awareness* consists of courage, faith in yourself, and commitment to mindfulness practice itself. The way of awareness thrives upon a great curiosity about what life is really about. It encourages you to ask: What could life be like when experienced free of the prison of reaction to anxiety, fear, and panic? What is living like when free of the determination to feel only the pleasant things and to make war on anything that feels different or unpleasant?

The way of awareness is nourished by the power of radical acceptance and compassion for all experience arising in your consciousness.

And, most of all, the way of awareness depends on you to *remember*, moment by moment, and to pay attention with affection and mercy.

A GIFT FOR YOURSELF AND OTHERS

In doing the meditations and practices in this book, you are also invited to remember that it is not only for yourself that you practice and seek freedom from fears and anxiety. For a world as troubled, frightened, and filled with hatred as ours, the peace and wisdom you find in your practice of mindfulness, kindness, and compassion will be a blessing, and welcome medicine for many others.

May you and the world benefit from your practice.

the foundation

We live in the present moment.

In this very moment you have within you the possibility and the necessary ingredients to transform your experience of life in all of its expressions, including the joys and fears, and the pain and pleasures.

Through the softness and gentleness of simple noticing—without judgment and with affection and mercy for your inner and outer experience—you can begin to realize a deeper connection and awaken to a wiser understanding of who you are and what life actually offers.

YOUR DIRECT EXPERIENCE OF MEDITATION IS WHAT REALLY MATTERS

These daily meditations offer a wide variety of ways to use your innate capacity for sensitive attention and compassionate awareness in order to help you embrace your full potential in being human. In this book, that full range of human experience expressly includes learning new ways of meeting and managing the demanding and upsetting energies of fear, worry, and anxiety.

To fully appreciate your wholeness and possibility as a human being, it is crucial to learn the language and skills of awareness and of kind, compassionate attention. The practice and actual experience of yourself as present, aware, and openhearted will tell you more about who you are than any particular experience, including difficult ones.

To fully benefit from the possibilities in these practices, therefore, you have to actually *do* the meditations! It is not enough to just *read* them, although that in itself can be helpful.

Some Initial Practical Points About Doing Your Meditations

In meditation, it is most helpful if you *cultivate the habit of practicing your meditations no matter how you are feeling.* Excited, bored, sleepy, anxious, it doesn't matter—just do it!

And *practice without requiring anything special to happen or anything to change.* "Not judging" and "not striving" thus become immediate practice allies and attitudes that support you.

Be sure to *give yourself the time and space you need for your meditation practice to unfold.* This means doing some practice daily, either as formal meditation or informally in the moments of waiting and moving through your day.

Make your meditation your friend and ally, and take it with you wherever you go. By weaving your daily meditations into the fabric of everyday life, you give your practice its best chance to flower, and yourself the best chance to discover your true possibilities for transformation and healing in the myriad situations that living brings.

It is only through regular meditation practice—in good times and bad—that you will develop your art and skills in meditation and will learn your real capacity and ability to meet even the most difficult challenges with fresh eyes and deep awareness.

Walking through the valley of the shadow of fear, anxiety, and even death, how can you expect to *suddenly* remember your wholeness and strength? Where will you find comfort in that moment if you have not found it before?

Each moment that you practice meditation, you are preparing to face life's greatest demands with mindful presence, gratitude, courage, wisdom, and compassion.

Each time you practice in the face of some form of resistance or mind-habit of inattention and doubt, recognizing it, not yielding but staying present with interest and sensitivity, you actually empower yourself to face and cope skillfully with the most difficult situations (as well as the most joyful ones) you will encounter.

So that is why we say you have to actually *do* the practices. Your life really could depend on it!

THE BUILDING BLOCKS IN YOUR FOUNDATION

There are some basic "building blocks"—concepts and suggestions—that can make a huge difference in how you benefit from and use this book. You might think of this section as a kind of "owner's manual" for using the daily meditations.

In the remainder of this section, you will find information that provides a larger context for meditation and health, for understanding anxiety, and for the basic practices of mindfulness, kindness, and compassion that you will use throughout this book. You may wish to revisit this section from time to time as you get to know the daily meditations and make them a part of your life.

You Are More Than Your Thoughts, Feelings, and Reactions

When you practice mindfulness—the art of friendly and "allowing" attention to the flow of experience through the present moment—you immediately begin to notice that thoughts are happening, sensations are changing, and reactions to experiences around you are forming in your mind and body.

Noticing this changing flow opens you to the realization that thoughts, feelings, and reactions are *not* your identity!

People say things like, "I am an anxious person," "I am not kind enough," and so on, as if qualities and conditions like anxiety and kindness are permanent and are identities in themselves. Practicing mindfulness, you quickly see that even intimate, intense experiences and energies like anxiety, fear, and panic are not your permanent identity. You know this because you can hold them in awareness and see them change and eventually leave you. Knowing they are *not* you immediately gives you a different and powerful way to relate to any of those experiences whenever one comes to visit, here, in the present moment.

Understanding More About Anxiety

Anxiety is the fear reaction—without a threat that justifies the intensity of the fear or without a clear threat at all. Anxiety can be persistent and chronic as well as acute. Worry is the thinking mind's way of manifesting anxiety by repeating stories and thoughts that feed and fuel the fear reaction.

The causes of anxiety and its expression in mind and body are complex and remain incompletely understood. However, a good overview of current knowledge about anxiety is summarized by Edmund Bourne, Ph.D., in his popular book *The Anxiety and Phobia Workbook*, fourth edition (Bourne 2005). Dr. Bourne notes that anxiety has predisposing causes, triggers, and maintaining causes. In other words, a person can have a *predisposition* to anxiety that is rooted somewhat in their biology as well as in the conditions and family life in which they were raised. Conditions that seem to associate with anxiety later in life include having close family members who are anxious, parents who are overly controlling and critical, and living in conditions that foster emotional insecurity and suppress healthy self-assertiveness.

When this predisposition meets certain *triggers*, a person can experience anxiety in a variety of forms. Common triggers include important loss, significant life change, exposure to certain drugs, and traumatic experience.

When the trigger has evoked anxiety, then *maintaining causes* can become operational to sustain or even worsen the intensity and/or frequency and duration of anxiety's expression. Typical maintaining causes include repeatedly avoiding the trigger; developing inner self-talk that is anxious, self-critical, and based in mistaken beliefs; not knowing how or not taking time to relax mind and body and to engage in fun activities; and not having a supportive foundation or belief system that provides the perspective of a greater meaning and purpose to your life.

There is growing evidence that meditation practices can enable you to relax mind and body, soothe and comfort yourself, and recognize and break free of the inner habits of self-talk and self-criticism that may be maintaining anxiety and worry. Meditation practices have also long been recognized for their ability to enrich our lives and illuminate meaning and purpose by focusing attention and attuning it to the present moment.

Meditation as Medicine

Meditation, in its variety of forms, represents an ancient "inner technology" whose benefits are being rediscovered and further illuminated by modern science. In addition to a growing body of scientific medical research (which is beyond the scope of this volume to detail), several recent popular books have summarized modern scientific findings about meditation practices in an effort to understand the benefits attributed to meditation.

Jon Kabat-Zinn's books, especially *Full Catastrophe Living* (2005) and *Coming to Our Senses* (2005), explain the healing and liberating role of mindfulness in a wide variety of stress- and health-related conditions.

Daniel Goleman's narration of a scientific dialogue with the Dalai Lama, *Destructive Emotions* (2003), recounts how modern science has demonstrated that awareness-training strategies such as meditation can strengthen emotional stability and enhance positive moods.

Sharon Begley's book, *Train Your Mind, Change Your Brain* (2007), describes state-of-the-art neuroscience that shows how meditation practices, long described as "training" for mind and heart, can actually evoke measurable and sustainable changes in the brain. This capacity of the brain to alter its structure is called *neuroplasticity* and is a concept at the cutting edge of current neuroscience and psychology.

Daniel J. Siegel, in his book *The Mindful Brain* (2007), reviews current findings on mindfulness and its ability to enhance physical, mental, and social well-being, and suggests that mindfulness practice stimulates "resonance circuits" in the brain to grow in ways that transform moment-to-moment states of awareness into longer-term, more durable forms of resilience.

In all of these works there is a familiar theme: for any benefit to arise from meditation, you have to *do* the meditation. Just as any good medicine only works when you take it, so meditation can only help you if you practice it!

Suggestions for Practicing Meditation

In using these daily meditations, or doing any other meditation practice you may already have, it can be helpful to keep some additional practical points about practicing meditation in mind.

FORMAL AND INFORMAL PRACTICE

It is important to weave meditation into your life both formally and informally. *Formal practice* is simply doing meditation as your primary activity for a dedicated period of time. For example, you may want to give yourself fifteen to thirty minutes of protected time to explore and deepen your practice, using any of the particular meditation methods that resonate with you.

Informal practice means bringing meditative awareness or a specific practice into the flow of daily life. For example, while stuck in traffic you could do mindful breathing or a loving-kindness meditation. Or while waiting for an appointment or for a friend, you could practice mindful listening or tune in mindfully to your body.

By developing your meditation skills in both formal and informal settings, you will learn what it means to have meditation as your friend and ally.

HOW LONG SHOULD YOU MEDITATE?

Even a little bit of meditation can be good for you. There are studies that report benefits for people who do formal meditation for anywhere from twenty to forty-five minutes daily. And experienced meditators and those on intensive meditation retreats routinely meditate formally for an hour or longer at a time.

But don't be intimidated by these examples. Meditation can be like an exercise program for your body in that you may need to build up your concentration and strength of presence slowly with repeated sessions. So start with a few minutes and work your way up to a comfortable period for practice.

Try to get to the place where you can practice for twenty or thirty minutes on an almost daily basis. This will open up more possibilities for you in terms of doing different and longer practices.

WHEN, WHERE, AND HOW?

For formal practice time, it is very helpful to make an approximate time and have an actual place with necessary supports for privacy, comfortable sitting or lying down, and a way to listen to any meditation instructions you may need. You may also wish to have some inspirational objects or pictures around the place in which you meditate, or some books or a journal to record your experiences. (Of course, remember that you are there to meditate, so don't let the books or objects distract you from that!)

As your experience builds, you will become comfortable meditating in a wide variety of places and situations. But if you are just starting, it is wise to give yourself as much friendly support as possible to build healthy habits of meditation. By establishing a supportive and safe environment for your meditation, you take a giant step toward having a strong meditation practice.

USING GUIDED MEDITATIONS VS. GUIDING YOURSELF

The meditations in this book, as well as many others you may encounter, could be considered "guided" in that they offer rather specific instructions. Listening to guided meditations can be a very good way to explore different methods and practices of meditation.

In fact, a good way to work with the meditations in this book could be to have someone read them to you as you practice, or to record them for yourself, pausing and reading slowly through each line, and then listening and practicing by following the recorded instructions.

At some point, most people who practice meditation do not rely on guided meditations. They settle on one or more specific practices and work with them until they have enough confidence and comfort to do "their" meditation any place and any time they like. You may want to select one or more meditations in this book for use that way. They can become your basic practice and a kind of anchor for you to steady your meditation wherever you go.

It can be especially valuable for you to develop a basic mindfulness practice (of breathing or walking, for example) that you can turn to whenever you wish, in any situation. Learning and trusting your ability to be mindful will support you in any other meditation method or situation you meet.

ATTITUDE: YOUR MOST IMPORTANT INGREDIENT

When all is said and done, it is likely that the most important thing about meditation is your attitude. There are many ways to say it, for example, you have heard "nonstriving" and "nonjudging" before in this book; but practicing with a wise and skillful attitude cannot be overstated.

Practice your meditation with curiosity and an open heart, not with any overt or hidden agenda. Drop any sense of meditating "in order to" make anything special happen or to make anything change. Just practice. Pay attention without requiring things to be the way your thinking mind wants or says they "should" be.

If you bring such interest, curiosity, and "not-knowing" to your meditation, whether it is formal or informal, you give yourself the best possibility of reaping the true benefits of meditation.

THE ATTITUDINAL FOUNDATION
OF MINDFULNESS

Being mindful means paying attention on purpose with an open mind and an open heart. It means a kind of noticing with a radical acceptance that does not require what you notice to change in any way. And this noticing is centered here, in the present moment.

You already have the necessary ingredients to be mindful. And you can strengthen your capacity for mindfulness through practice, which is what many of the meditations in this book are about.

In developing mindfulness practices for stress reduction and health (the MBSR model mentioned earlier), Jon Kabat-Zinn named seven factors or attitudes that support mindfulness practice as he (and others) taught it in his clinic. You might think of these attitudes as a kind of "heart" of mindfulness, because they point to aspects of our wholeness as human beings and to the possibility of greater fullness and depth in our attention.

The seven attitudinal factors Kabat-Zinn named as the foundation of mindfulness practice are nonjudging, patience, beginner's mind, trust, nonstriving, acceptance, and letting go. It can be good to know about these factors as you build your own practice.

While you have heard a bit already about *nonjudging*, and *nonstriving*, it is useful to know that *patience* includes patience with yourself and your mind's unruly and restless movement while you are meditating and to know that *beginner's mind* means to bring attention to each moment and to each experience, even to each breath, as if you have never seen it before: "not-knowing" about it, curious and welcoming. *Trust* is about trusting yourself to be able to be present and stay present, to pay attention, and to actually know what is happening in this moment. *Acceptance* means a willingness (without necessarily liking it) to see things exactly as they are in this moment—which is the basis for true change and healing. And *letting go* means not following or fighting experience that comes into your awareness, but letting it go.

So as you practice paying attention on purpose—being mindful—recall these attitudes and actually include them as a foundation of your moment-by-moment way of being present with attention. If you do, these attitudes will reward you richly.

THE IMPORTANCE OF KINDNESS AND COMPASSION

Kindness is a quality of heart that is friendly. Kindness wishes well, wishes happiness and ease, and wishes peace and good health. Being kind enables you to welcome experience.

Compassion is the feeling of being moved by the pain in a situation and the desire to help. Compassion carries with it a willingness to remain present to pain in the hope of giving aid or some measure of relief.

Mindfulness— the awareness that arises from a nonjudging, allowing attention—actually contains the energies of kindness and compassion. Your ability to be "mindful" of difficult feelings like fear and anxiety depends directly on the qualities of kindness and compassion present as you pay attention.

Another way to put this connection between kindness, compassion, and awareness is to ask the question, "How are you treating life?" When you are "making war" on something, including an unpleasant feeling like anxiety, it is very difficult to be mindful of the experience. When attention is driven by hostility and aversion, then the quality of awareness that follows, and the wisdom and understanding, healing and transformation possible in the moment, are probably being blocked.

And the habits of making war, of a dislike for and aversion to disturbing experiences, are deep and strong. The habits can be unconscious also. So without realizing it, even while paying attention to them, you can be fighting anxiety or fear or pain or grief, and judging yourself harshly as you do so.

Only by being willing to adopt a stance of *radical acceptance*, of actually allowing and welcoming the full range of your experience, can you realize the true power of mindfulness to free you from deep habits of reactivity to difficult experiences.

Section 3 of this book, Daily Meditations for Befriending Your Anxious Mind and Body, is devoted to exploring the attitudes of kindness and compassion explicitly. By learning to cultivate attitudes of kindness and compassion to others and to yourself and your own pain, you can strengthen mindfulness and move beyond the restricting and confining habits of hatred and aversion that block your perception and experience of the fullness of the present moment.

DEVELOPING WISDOM AND EQUANIMITY

If mindfulness is about "being, not doing" (with respect to the experience happening in the present moment), you might also say that "being informs doing" (that is, being mindful leads to more effective choices and happier outcomes).

More effective "doing" then comes directly from the understanding and wisdom that arise from seeing clearly what is actually happening. For example, caught in a storm of worry and anxiety when facing a party or other social situation, you could be "unmindful" and remain in the old habits of "doing"—all the thinking and feeling patterns that sustain and even increase the anxiety. Fighting the distress by proliferating the usual thought chains of doubt and explanations (or engaging in old and desperate behaviors) is only likely to worsen the situation or to distract you temporarily, at best.

However, if you can manage to stop this reactive, habitual "doing" and just "be" with the experience of the moment, using attention, radical acceptance, kindness, and compassion, then you may notice that something very different happens.

Understanding and wisdom arise as you pay attention more closely.

The intensity of the distress may shift, but more importantly, by being mindful, your relationship to the intensity shifts. You begin to experience yourself as separate from the difficult, painful feelings and can perhaps notice that there are a variety of possibilities and choices present in the moment.

You may even find yourself acting on a possibility previously unseen or unsuspected.

For example, in the situation of the anxiety about the party, through mindful attention to your own inner life, you may notice a mean and critical inner voice berating you about your social skills and attractiveness. Upon noticing this voice, you may choose consciously to ignore it or to offer yourself an affirmation or to give yourself some other reassurance. Armed with more support, you can then meet your situation more effectively and happily. And the next time the mean voice arises, you can remember how you handled it successfully this time and therefore be more confident.

In this way, the willingness to "be" with what is happening for even a few moments—paying attention on purpose with radical acceptance—then reveals a better, more effective way to "do" what comes next, even in a difficult situation.

Equanimity is the steadiness and brightness of mind and heart that allows you to face any situation with equal courage and to remain equally close to unfolding experience, regardless of what it is. Equanimity is not based in willpower or determination so much as it arises naturally from the understanding and wisdom that comes from repeated experiences of staying present and open to changing conditions inside and outside of you.

As you experience your capacity to stay present and the benefits of "being, not doing," the truth that you are not your thoughts, feelings, and upset (and the changing nature of those conditions) can lead you to have greater faith and courage and increased steadiness whenever those conditions return to visit you in the present moment.

As you work with the daily meditations in this book, you may discover that wisdom and equanimity support you in surprising ways. Notice how your concepts and experience of wisdom and equanimity shift and grow as you move more deeply into these meditations and practices.

BASIC INSTRUCTIONS FOR BREATHING MINDFULLY

Breathe mindfully for a few moments.

You will see this instruction, or a variation of it, many times in these daily meditations. Mindful breathing is an invitation and a means to collect yourself, with sensitive and welcoming attention, here, in the present moment.

By putting attention deliberately on your natural process and sensations of breathing, you come immediately into the present moment and step back from reacting and identifying with the habitual, and usually unconscious, stream of inner thoughts and feelings.

One outcome of mindful breathing is that you are immediately more open to and aware of what is happening inside and outside of you. And this awareness then becomes the basis for seeing and acting in new and more effective ways.

The following are simple instructions for mindful breathing. You will find variations in some of the practices in the book. Work with any instructions that resonate for you. Make them your own. You will not be sorry!

1. *Whenever you wish to practice breathing mindfully, in any physical position you are in, begin by gently putting attention on your body, noticing, as you do, the sensations and position of arms, legs, torso, head, and face. Let the body sensations come and go. Let your body relax. Allow any areas of holding or contraction in your body to soften and open as much as they can, safely.*

2. *As your body settles and relaxes more, allow your attention to come to rest at the place in your body where you can feel the sensations of your breath coming in and going out most easily. Perhaps that place is at the tip of your nose or it's your chest or your abdomen. No place is better than another. All are good. Rest your attention at the place in your body where it is easiest for you to feel the breath sensations coming and going.*

3. *Notice the breath sensations directly—expansion, contraction, soft, deep, and so on. Let your body breathe naturally without trying to control the breath in any way. Just pay attention and allow yourself to feel the sensations as they come to you and as they leave you.*

4. *As you notice the breath sensations, you may notice a small space at the end of the in breath and a longer one at the end of the out breath. If you like, you can rest in that space and notice how the breath sensations arise and return to the still, silent space. You can let the steadiness and stillness fill you as breath sweeps through you.*

5. *As you practice letting the breath sensations come and go, feeling them with increasing sensitivity, you may notice your mind wanders to other sensations, to sounds, or to thoughts or feelings. When this happens, you have not done anything wrong. Be kind and patient with yourself. Notice where your attention moved. You have not made a mistake. The moving attention is only your mind doing what all minds do.*

6. *Gently bring your attention back to the breath sensations whenever your attention wanders. You don't have to fight or struggle to do this. Simply let the breath back "in" to be with you here, in this moment. Noticing softly and gently the sensations of this breath, now, let the breath sensations back "in" as often as you need to.*

7. *As you practice, you may notice your mind is busy with thoughts. That is okay. Thoughts are not the enemy. You do not have to fight them and you do not have to follow them, either. Treat thoughts like anything else that draws your attention. Notice them, allow them to be as they are, and gently let your attention open back to, and settle on, the breath sensations.*

8. *As your practice continues, you may find that a sense of inner space and stillness deepens, opens around, and contains all of your unfolding experience, including thoughts, feelings, sensations, and sounds. Practice resting in that space. Let all of the experiences come and go through the spaciousness, along with your breath sensations. Let yourself abide, in stillness and spaciousness, in the present moment, alert,*

sensitive, welcoming, and undisturbed by your unfolding and changing experience.

9. *Practice for as long as you like and as often as you like. Practice for different periods of time and in different circumstances.*

10. *End your practice by opening your eyes if they are closed, and moving gently.*

USING THESE "DAILY MEDITATIONS"

Looking back on what has been said, and looking ahead to doing the daily meditations, it could be helpful to review and recall some major points:

- Give yourself time every day to practice and explore the power of meditation, both formally and informally. Give yourself the opportunity for healing and transformation through meditation by being consistent and dedicated in your practice, regardless of how you feel or what is happening.

- You don't have to do or like all the meditations in this book! You don't have to do them in any order, either. However, if you want to promote healing and transformation in your life, you must do something!

- It will help to become well acquainted with the major themes in this book.

- These themes are supporting feelings of safety and ease, establishing mindfulness in different situations, cultivating a kind and compassionate attitude toward self and others, and recognizing the larger patterns of interconnection and meaning that are present in moment-by-moment experiences.

- Give yourself plenty of time with these themes and the meditations in each chapter. Read them and reflect, and "try them on" repeatedly. Take them with you and try them in different situations.

- Remember that attitude is important. Be nonstriving and nonjudging, friendly, and curious!

Let go of trying to change anything or to make anything happen when you practice. Let go of judging yourself or the "results" of your meditation. Instead, use the time and place you give yourself for daily practice, including the "informal" spaces, to get to know the themes, the practices, and how they work together with each other, and in your life, with its changing conditions.

As you get a feel for the themes and the different possibilities offered in the wide variety of practices, work more deeply with the practices and themes that resonate and call to you most clearly and warmly. Notice how your choice of practice may change from day to day or week to week. Let yourself be curious and experimental as you explore and attend more closely to the meditation choices and the changing landscapes of your inner and outer worlds.

As you move more deeply into the language and skills of inner awareness, it may be helpful to keep a journal or diary of your experiences, insights, and questions.

We strongly encourage you to put particular energy into developing a basic practice of mindfulness (such as mindful breathing). Learn to trust in your ability to establish mindfulness in different situations. Take an interest in exploring the deeper territory of formal practice using mindfulness of breathing, body sensations, thoughts, feelings, or mindfulness of the recognition of changing conditions and stillness in meditation. You will find instructions for mindfulness of all of these conditions within the diverse meditations in this book.

Finally, remember that you are learning to see and relate in new ways. Have patience and kindness for yourself, and indulge in curiosity and a sense of wonder and awe for whatever arises.

See if you can learn to bring the same kind of attention and affection to the rest of your life that you bring to your meditation. The benefits might astound you, and the world will thank you.

daily meditations for relaxing and feeling safe

Today, when strong feelings disturb me, including anxiety, worry, or fear, I will acknowledge those feelings consciously with compassion and will practice relaxing and nurturing the experience of calm and safety in my mind and body.

IN THIS SECTION

The meditations and practices in this section are invitations to explore your capacity for calming and soothing body and mind. They all begin with the elements of mindful attention and an intention to turn toward and embrace conditions that support peace and ease within you.

Feelings of anxiety, fear, and worry are not you, yet they are very intense and distracting. When the body's alarm system has turned on, the "fear body" becomes a demanding visitor in the present moment as well. And remember that your fear body arises whether the "threat" is believed to be outside of it or comes from frightening thoughts generated in your mind.

In such times of upset, and in other moments as well, it is very useful to know how to activate your built-in capacity for calm and ease. As human beings we all have a hardwired system in us to produce relaxation as well as a system that produces the stress reaction, the fight-or-flight response.

You can activate your relaxation response by directing attention and by skillful use of thoughts and images. Your body knows how to do the rest!

As you do the other practices in the different sections of this book, you will appreciate more and more how the natural capacity for ease and relaxation arises in mind and body even as you do those practices. While relaxation is not a measure or the ultimate goal of mindfulness practice, a degree of calm and ease is a great support for mindfulness and for the wisdom and understanding that follow from mindful attention.

AS YOU PRACTICE

Some "pearls" may be useful to keep in mind as you do these practices specifically:

- *You don't have to fight your fear and worry; simply stop feeding it.* Just abandon it by "walking away" and shifting your focus of attention as the meditations instruct.

- *You are more than your fear and worry.* In these meditations and practices, you are learning to trust that you have a great heart and intelligence within that is capable of holding spaciously and kindly even feelings of upset. All of the meditations and practices in this book point you back to your wholeness—that which is more than any momentary experience or unpleasant energy you are feeling.

- *Pay attention to any feelings you have that are actually uncomfortable with being "too relaxed."* These are not unusual, and if you pay attention when they arise, you may be able to recognize familiar mental stories and thoughts that make you actually resist becoming as relaxed as you could be. Getting to know such stories and thoughts is an important beginning to becoming free from them.

- *Finally, in doing all the meditations and practices in this section and throughout this book, remember there is a paradox at work.* The meditations and practices are most powerful when you aren't trying to use them to make anything happen at all!

So don't *try* to relax. Don't keep asking, "Is it working?" And definitely don't try to make the intense and unpleasant feelings go away.

Just move your attention from wherever it is and focus more sharply on following the particular instructions for the practice or meditation you have chosen. Remember that non-judging, nonstriving, and allowing are at the heart of mindfulness practice.

keep in mind

- Attention and awareness are *not* anxiousness or upset.

- *You* are not the feelings of upset, either.

- There is a much larger, stronger quality to your wholeness that permits it to safely contain any momentary energy like anxiety, fear, pain, or worry.

- As you learn to trust your deep inner capacity for relaxation and for presence, you will feel more confident and safer facing whatever challenges life brings you.

equanimity: finding peace within the process of life

Equanimity has a mysterious and powerful quality of steadiness and imperturbability in the face of challenges and change. Yet equanimity is rooted not in gritting your teeth and stubborn willpower, but in the wisdom and openness of heart that follows acceptance of the inevitability of change at every level.

Let this practice be a thoughtful reflection, or a meditation, accompanied by mindful breathing, to bring you equanimity.

You may want to take a few moments and breathe mindfully or relax and soothe yourself before engaging these reflections. Experiment, and explore them, focusing on one or two phrases, breathing mindfully, and noticing what thoughts and feelings arise in you.

Remember, this meditation is not about "getting it right" but about discovery and wisdom.

Filled with fear, may I recognize the universe rising to greet and comfort me.

Burning with anger, may I recall the dignity of others.

Despairing at my own weakness and vulnerability, may I remember how every life contains these things.

Aching with pain and loneliness, may I hold myself in love and compassion.

Brimming with happiness, may I bathe in it—and freely let it go.

Speaking with absolute certainty, may my next remark be laughter at myself.

Wait!

Allowing change completely, do I glimpse something else, something reassuring and safe, and always here?

working with this meditation

- As a meditative reflection, in a time of "formal" meditation, when you are steady and focused, try dropping one or more of these phrases into your awareness deliberately and listening for all the ripples that return.

- As a theme for investigation, try carrying a phrase or two into your day, post them where you will see them repeatedly, and let them illuminate different situations you face.

2.

sail away

Your critical inner voice can sabotage a perfectly good day. This voice has a tendency to become a blaring loudspeaker drowning out whatever sense of confidence you might have. Your inner monologue scrutinizes everything by saying such things as, "You shouldn't do this; you'll hurt yourself" or "You could be wrong about that; don't trust yourself" or "You don't know anything, so just give it up!"

Let's try visualization for quieting this overanalyzing negative talk, which will, in turn, restore your self-confidence and inner trust.

1. *While seated comfortably, rest your eyes and connect with your breath.*

2. *Imagine that you are sitting at the grassy edge of a small, gently rolling stream. You've come to this little babbling brook to take this moment to acknowledge your negative inner self-talk and be mindful of what it says, how it says it, and the subtleties of language and tone that it conveys to you. This voice knows your every fear and worry at all times. Make a mental list of some of those fears and worries that are surfacing right now.*

3. *Now imagine each fear and worry being inscribed into the surface of a fallen leaf. Each leaf will represent your collection of sabotaging thoughts that prevent you from feeling secure.*

4. *Once you have a good-sized pile of worry leaves, pick them up one by one and set them carefully on the surface of the water, allowing the current to take them away. You are letting your critical thoughts and doubts wash downstream, moving further away from you with each passing moment. As you look downstream, you can hardly see what remains of those fleeting, distant uncertainties that once held you back with insecurity. Observe them until they are completely out of sight.*

5. *When you're ready, open your eyes, stretch your limbs, and return to the present moment.*

3.

befriend your panic

Leaving a place of security, such as your home or any place familiar and safe, can be agonizing, filling you with panic and a sense of dread. Panic can manifest as a fluttering of your heart, shortness of breath, or tensing of your muscles. Panic can be physically paralyzing. Perhaps you're required to go somewhere for work that you've never been or perhaps you suddenly become overwhelmed with a feeling of being very far away from a safe place.

Your panic represents your fear that you are not safe. Panic can lead to thoughts of wanting to run, hide, or collapse. When panic sets in, meditation and mindfulness can be your friend and a tool to help you feel calm again.

1. *Take this moment to sit with your panicky feelings and tell yourself that your fears are precious reminders to be gentle with yourself. There's no need to berate or punish yourself for these worrisome feelings.*

2. *This meltdown will pass as you allow your mind to remember the places where you do feel safe and sound. Make a mental or written list of those spaces, such as your bedroom, backyard, car, best friend's garden, favorite restaurant, and*

so on. Try to visualize yourself in one of these places. Carry this feeling of safety into the space where you are now.

3. *Now try to picture yourself standing tall, confident, and trusting these new uncertain surroundings. You are accomplishing your task in this new place. You are trusting yourself to do the next right thing. You are finding the strength to complete what you started.*

4. *Consider ways that you might be able to comfort yourself right now. Perhaps give yourself a slight hug, remember to breathe, or call a friend who is good at reassuring you during a crisis.*

4.

breath and light: a meditation for deeply relaxing body and mind

Allow yourself at least twenty to thirty minutes to work through your entire body doing this meditation. You may also do the basic practice for specific parts and regions of your body in shorter periods.

This meditation can be done lying down or sitting comfortably. If you choose to lie down, be alert for the tendency to fall asleep. However, if you really need the sleep, relax and enjoy it!

1. *Take a comfortable position and breathe mindfully, with close attention to your breath sensations, for several minutes.*

2. *As you attend to the breath, allow your mind to slow down, going slower, slower, and slower. For the time of this meditation, there is nowhere else to go and nothing else to do.*

3. *Imagine you are resting in a radiant cloud of beautiful white light. The light has a slight glow, a quality of soothing warmth, and you immediately know that it is friendly and kind.*

4. *Move your attention to your head.*

5. *As you breathe in, imagine you are inviting the beautiful light to flow into your head, filling and surrounding every part and space—your skull, eyes, mouth, nose, and so on. Let the light and the breath saturate every cell and tissue and space they touch.*

6. *As you breathe out, imagine the breath carries away all unnecessary stress and tension in your head and all of its parts and spaces, leaving behind ease and relaxation.*

7. *When your attention wanders or thoughts arise, you have not done anything wrong or made a mistake. Just notice where your attention went, and let the light and breath touch that place as well. You might even allow any thoughts to dissolve into the light.*

8. *Gently bring attention back to your head and continue mindful breathing and your focus on the image of the light.*

9. *When you are ready to move on, in a relaxed and unhurried way, shift attention to your neck and shoulders, and let the breath bring the light there. Let each out breath carry away unnecessary stress and tension just as you did with your head.*

10. *Stay with your neck and shoulders as long as you like.*

11. *When you are ready to move on, move to your hands and arms, including your fingers.*

12. *Next, bring breath and light mindfully and softly through your torso, front and back, and deeply inside the chest and abdomen.*

13. *When you are ready, leave the torso, and move on in succession to the pelvis, the legs, and the feet and toes.*

14. *Pausing and breathing mindfully in each region, let the light suffuse and fill every cell and tissue. Explore the depths of your inner body, feeling the flow of sensations, vibrations, the sense of hardness, temperature, moisture, and even the movement of air.*

15. *Throughout, relax and let the breath and the light support you.*

16. *If you cannot feel a part or region, relax. Breathe there anyway. Invite the light in. Move on after a few breaths.*

17. *Whenever you become distracted, relax and notice. Let breath and light ease the distraction. Gently bring attention back to the region of your body you are working with, or simply rest on the sensations of your breathing for a few breaths more.*

18. *When you have moved through your entire body, let yourself rest with breath and light moving through your entire body as well. Breathe mindfully, bathing in the light as long as you wish.*

19. *Let stillness, relaxation, and mindfulness of breath and body heal and restore you.*

safety shield

When you were a child, your parents likely reminded you daily that "Safety comes first," "Accidents do happen," and "You can never be too careful." Today this desire for safety and protection may inhibit you from doing normal, fun activities that other people can enjoy without hesitation or fear. Maybe you avoid swimming for fear of drowning or you don't drive on freeways for fear of other cars speeding by or you turn down invitations for travel and adventure to new places because you don't want to leave your city. The unknown lurks behind every situation and seizes your ability to relax and enjoy life.

Try this mindfulness exercise to quell this fear and cultivate an openness for adventure.

1. *Be aware of what is making you feel unsafe. Take notice of why you may feel concern about this particular situation that you are facing. What feels dangerous or unpredictable about it? Has this situation come up in the past? Does it come up regularly? What other feelings accompany it?*

2. *Take this moment to get visually creative and design your own circle of protection. Your safety shield can extend any distance that you desire—ten feet or ten miles—it's up to*

you. What special features does your protective sphere have? What color is it?

3. Once your safety shield is up, say aloud or to yourself, "I am safe and secure in this place. No harm can come to me. I am protected from danger. I am free to experience pleasurable events and I will be okay."

4. Your surrounding safety armor can be taken with you wherever you go—supermarket, party, swimming pool—and it can be retrieved instantly by simply meditating on a circle that engulfs you and your surroundings in a protective shield.

roadway to serenity

Due to a very serious car accident that occurred during a rainstorm many years ago, a dear friend cannot drive on freeways in the rain without experiencing terrifying anxiety. She is afraid of hydroplaning, losing control of her car, being swept across multiple lanes, and crashing into other cars. Though she has an excellent driving record and has not since been involved in an accident, she is still unable to feel safe on the highway when it's raining.

Whether you're driving or biking or walking, when feelings of safety are questioned, you may lose all sense of reality. Perhaps you may have felt this way in a similar situation in your life.

The next time you experience anxiety like this, try this exercise to help you cope when reeling thoughts of endangerment overwhelm you.

1. *Give yourself permission to stop what you're doing, for example, by pulling over to the side of the road or finding a place to sit, undistracted by your previous activity.*

2. *Acknowledge the possible spiraling thoughts and feelings of worry and trepidation that you are facing right now. You may have a constant running tape loop of possible dreadful*

scenarios. *Perhaps you fear that you might kill another driver or passenger or perhaps that you might hurt yourself. Often these images of distressing outcomes are endless and unrelenting. Let them arise and then let them go.*

3. *Quiet your mind by letting your thoughts come and go without trying to take action. Take this time to recognize that in this very moment you are alive and well, healthy and resilient, safe and sound. No one has been harmed, and nothing has been damaged.*

4. *Say aloud or to yourself, "I am not in an accident. No one is hurt. I am not at risk for endangering myself or anyone else. I am presently secure and protected from any possible threat or danger."*

5. *As you contemplate returning to your task at hand, be mindful of all the little things around you that you are not afraid of. Rain itself is Mother Nature's way of watering her garden and beautifying the earth. The clouds overhead will pass and release the sun's gentle warmth once again. The freeway is your constant traveling companion that guides you just where you need to be each day.*

You can now return to driving, feeling confident and secure.

just the wind blowing: allowing life to move through this moment

This meditation can be a good practice to do when you are either relaxed or upset. The more you practice "feeling the wind blowing," the more help this meditation will be for you when facing any situation or challenge.

1. *Take a comfortable position.*

2. *Bring mindful attention to your breath, feeling it deeply and completely in your body. Steady your focus and attention by placing attention on your breath for a few moments.*

3. *Relax and completely let go of trying to change anything or to make anything happen.*

4. *Now imagine that you are in a beautiful place in nature. Surrounded by beauty, you can feel the wind blowing around you.*

5. *Let all of your conscious experience—sounds, sensations, thoughts, emotions, everything—become the wind.*

6. *Feel all of it moving and changing, arriving, moving around and over you, and then going.*

7. *Notice how the wind takes on different qualities—soft, strong, harsh, gusty, gentle.*

8. *Relax as the wind blows around you. Let it come and go in all of its forms.*

9. *You remain here, in calmness, abiding.*

8.

sound track of life

Music nourishes your spirit, lifts your heart, touches your soul, and makes you want to sway to the rhythm of the beat. Music can move you to tears, stir up romantic memories, and inspire your creative side. Relaxing music can bring serenity to an anxious mind. You might consider making a CD mix of your favorite calming songs to keep on hand in the car or at work.

1. *For now, think of one or two restful tunes that you know have restored calm and balance for you in the past. You may even want to hum a few bars to yourself or pop in a particular CD if it is readily available.*

2. *Once you have a song in mind, take this time to just be in the quiet moment of the present. Why did you pick this special artist and song? Consider the recollections you attach to it. Pay attention to the subtle shifts in the pace, tempo, and cadence. Notice what instruments are easier to identify— flute, piano, guitar, drums. Focus on the melody, harmony, and composition, and reflect on other sensations that stir inside you. Do you tap your foot or feel like lying down, or does the song just make you smile? Open your heart to the*

vocals and lyrics; perhaps there is a hidden message tucked away just for you.

3. Take note of what kinds of feelings are surfacing for you—sorrow, joy, weariness, or contentment. Allow these mixed emotions to get swept up in the song, knowing that when the song ends, your emotions will untangle themselves and let you move more freely and calmly through your day. Let this song become the sound track of your life, a daily reminder that music can have a profoundly therapeutic and healing effect on your mind and body. Let this song be an invitation to dance with your soul without fear or worry to inhibit you.

calm in the eye of the storm

When in the throes of anxiety, you may feel like imminent danger and risk await you at every turn. Frightening thinking can erupt out of nowhere and nearly paralyze you with fear. It often begins with "what if" thoughts, such as "What if I hit that pedestrian?" "What if I have cancer?" "What if my coworkers see me panic and think I'm crazy?" "What if this elevator malfunctions, and we fall?" "What if my husband is hurt in a car accident?" This cycle of catastrophic thoughts distorts reality and makes it difficult to feel secure and to trust that you will survive.

This next meditation is an opportunity to replace fearful thoughts with more realistic ones that will allow your worries to dissipate.

1. *Take this moment to identify your frightening thoughts by making a mental or written list.*

2. *Ask yourself which fears have validity and which ones don't. Question how realistic your fears are. For example, if you are concerned about hitting someone with your car, ask yourself, "Have I ever hit anyone before?" It's very likely that you haven't, so there are good odds that you won't now. Or, for example, if you are terrified that a lingering flu bug*

might mean that you have a life-threatening illness, ask your-self, "What happened the last time I was sick?" Chances are your sore throat cleared up eventually, and gradually you felt better after some much-needed rest.

3. *Now make a new list of positive, hopeful, and realistic affir-mations to replace the old "what if" wheel of misfortune. Your affirmations might include the following: "I am an excellent and careful driver with a good driving record. I am confident in my ability to avoid danger." "I am strong and healthy. My body is capable of extraordinary healing." "My family and loved ones are safe and protected. Each night they return home safely."*

Consider keeping these affirmations on small index cards in your purse, briefcase, backpack, or somewhere readily available when you need them. These are your free tickets out of the tornado of anxiety.

noticing space, silence, and stillness: a meditation for opening heart and mind

By deliberately trying to see things in a new and fresh way, you can ease the grip of unconscious habits of perceiving, and of limited and restrictive views.

The following meditation invites you to look for the things often taken for granted. This "fresh" way of seeing can change everything! You can do this meditation anytime and anyplace. You can do this meditation as both a longer formal practice and as a shorter informal practice in different situations of daily living. Enjoy and grow with both approaches.

1. *Breathe mindfully for several breaths or longer.*

2. *Set an intention to see things freshly and to notice things differently. In this meditation, your focus will be on space, silence, and stillness.*

3. *Relax and look around mindfully. As you look, let go of stories and thoughts and let yourself see things directly, noticing shapes, color, light and dark, and movement.*

4. *When you are ready, deliberately shift your attention to the space around and between the objects you see. Notice how each object actually exists in a much larger container of empty space.*

5. *Watch the space, spaces around you, and things you see for as long as you like.*

6. *When you like, shift attention from watching space to listening mindfully to sounds.*

7. *Let your eyes close if it helps you focus on listening mindfully.*

8. *Notice how silence lives before, between, and after each sound. Let the sounds come and go as you focus more steadily on the silence. Rest with and in the silence.*

9. *When you are ready, leave the sounds and direct your attention to any thoughts or feelings you are having.*

10. *Notice the thoughts and feelings mindfully. Allow all the thoughts and feelings to come and go, not fighting or following them. Notice how they arise from and return to silence and stillness. Notice the space and stillness between the thoughts and feelings.*

11. *Breathe mindfully to steady and support your attention whenever you need to.*

12. *Notice the space, the silence, and the stillness whenever you like. It is always there to support you.*

II.

sensory scan

Given our economic climate, financial burdens, and skyrocketing layoffs, you may chronically worry about losing your job. Job instability can lead to fears of becoming homeless, hungry, and lost on the streets without any resources to keep you alive. Fears such as these may spiral into frenzied thoughts of future doom and neglect.

Let's let go of this "future-thinking" and concentrate on being present and mindful in this moment. Follow this meditation for returning to the present and letting go of the unknown future.

1. *Find a quiet space to sit and just be with yourself. While seated, close your eyes and rest your hands comfortably on your thighs.*

2. *Connect with your breath and imagine that each in breath energizes the body and each out breath relaxes the mind.*

3. *Engaging all of your senses, scan your immediate surroundings. What do you taste, hear, smell, feel, see, and sense? Can you hear the tip-tapping of computer keyboards at the office? Is the aftertaste of your orange-cranberry scone and coffee still in your mouth? Can you smell your partner's aftershave or*

perfume lingering from the hug you got this morning? Are you warmed up from the brisk walk from your car to your workplace? What other things do you notice?

Only a few moments ago, you were wrapped up in burdensome thoughts of what the future might or might not bring. Will you have a job tomorrow, next month, next year? Today you have a job. Today you are working and doing the best you can to maintain stability. Today the bills are paid and you are cared for. Let the power of your senses become creative tools for releasing you from the bondage of future-thinking. You are just here in this cathedral of spacious beauty and intrigue. This precious "now-moment" awaits you and can guide you to a place of gentle serenity any time you need it.

comforting companions

Generalizing can impair your stability and security. Perhaps you are prone to overexaggerate problems. For example, if you once caught a cold on an airplane, you decide never to fly again. Or if you experienced anxiety on an escalator, you avoid the escalator at all costs and only take the stairs. A single bad experience can tarnish how you react and feel about a similar situation in the future.

You may find yourself attaching "always" and "never" to your reactions: "I always feel that way." "I never do that." "This always happens to me." Your first clue to overgeneralizing is noticing the use of exaggerated terms, such as "massive," "huge," "awful," "always," "never," and so on.

The following meditation will help you to unravel your tendency to overexaggerate and to rediscover a more balanced reality.

1. *Make a mental or written list of a few of your inflated generalizations or oversimplifications. As you ponder this list, do not judge or criticize yourself. This list represents some of your coping strategies for avoiding anxiety and feeling safe.*

2. *Now take a moment to focus on things in your environment that make you feel safe and comforted. Perhaps it is your*

favorite coat or a bright, cloudless day or having your kids at home or dinner with your partner or having your dog or cat nearby or checking in with friends and loved ones over the phone.

Keep mental images of these things or moments that restore your feelings of security so that you can refer to them during times of unease and apprehension. These soothing remembrances can help restore your balance and calm. They are constant companions that remind you that comfort is not far away.

strong as a mountain

No matter how worried or anxious you feel, the earth remains here, beneath your feet. Mountains are also earth, solid and strong. Mountains endure and sustain. Their feet are deeply and broadly continuous with the earth. Whenever you feel like you have lost touch with your basic sense of strength and of feeling grounded, return to your mountain (and the earth) for support.

Doing this meditation can help you reconnect with your mountain and the earth.

1. *Take a comfortable position.*

2. *Breathe mindfully for a few minutes, growing more steady and present.*

3. *Expand your focus and include your body in mindful attention. Soften, open, and allow all of the vibrations, heaviness, contractions, and expansions as they appear, flow through, and depart the present moment.*

4. *Breathe mindfully and remain open and present to all changing sensations for a few more breaths.*

5. *Now visualize a mountain appearing in front of you. Let it be the most wonderful, inspiring mountain you have ever seen. Perhaps you have actually been there or perhaps you have only seen it in a photo or a film. Its very presence is soothing and reassuring.*

6. *Look more closely. Let the mountain reveal its details. Notice shapes and colors. Perhaps there are trees and grasses, or snow or great cliffs and jagged edges. Perhaps you notice boulders and barren spaces, or rich meadows filled with flowers. As you look more closely, you may even see clouds or rain or snow falling. You may find bright sunlight or haze or even fog.*

7. *Step back and appreciate the immensity and grandeur of your mountain. Feel its steadiness and majestic strength.*

8. *Notice how the mountain accepts changing conditions yet remains unmoved as people and animals, all types of weather, day and night, and all the seasons move over and around it.*

9. *Shift attention and focus again on the stillness and steadiness within yourself and your living, breathing body. Feel your own strength now. Let the mountain—accepting, steady, unshakable—be in you. Feel yourself become the mountain.*

10. *Try repeating the phrase "strong as a mountain" quietly to yourself, feeling the beauty and majesty of your heart, mind, and body, and your connectedness to the earth.*

14.

anywhere but here, please

Even when you are feeling strong, stable, and confident, there can be an ever-present, nagging worry that a full-blown anxiety attack could overcome you out of nowhere. Just the thought of having a major meltdown in public might prevent you from committing to certain activities, or you might back out of invitations to parties, small get-togethers, or even a date. It is not easy for others to understand what it is like for you to live with anxiety day in and day out.

This next visualization will assist you the next time you feel anxious in a social situation. You may want to make an audio recording of this meditation, speaking slowly and deliberately, pronouncing each word with clarity and calmness.

1. *Sink into a comfy chair or couch and let your mind and body go limp.*

2. *Concentrate for a few minutes on your breath and follow your body's natural breathing rhythm. Air whisks in, filling your lungs, and air whisks out, emptying your lungs. In this moment, you are grounding yourself to the most fundamental bodily function that keeps you alive—the breath.*

3. *You may have thoughts circulating through your mind— some benign and mundane, others disturbing and fretful. Let*

these contemplations come in and go out. Let them do their little dance in your brain. Observe these mental messages as if they were tiny dancers, twirling around each other, pirouetting to the right and left, whirling around and around without stopping. What are they saying? "I need a shower." "The dog hair needs to be vacuumed." "Who was I supposed to call back today?" "Did I pay that bill?" "I can't go to that dinner party; I might run into my ex and that would freak me out. What if I have a crazy meltdown in front of all those people? It would be a nightmare." "I have to go to my son's open house tonight, but what if I have an anxiety attack while I'm there?" "I have a presentation to give to the directors this week that I'm terrified about."

4. Let the thoughts come in and go out, much like your breathing . . . in and then out, in and then out, again.

5. Now imagine a time when you braved a public place and everything went just fine; in fact, maybe you had a terrific time. Where were you? Perhaps a wedding, baby shower, birthday party, or dinner with an old friend from out of town. What were you feeling on this occasion? Perhaps you felt tranquil, undisturbed by outside worries, and in your body. Imagine being back there now. You are relaxed, laughing about something familiar, and feeling comfortable in your surroundings. What are other people doing around you? Perhaps they are at ease, and some are smiling and engaging in light conversation.

6. Take this calming memory with you wherever you go to instill a feeling of security and self-assurance.

safe haven

If you experienced or witnessed a traumatic event in the past, you may have developed anxiety and other symptoms soon thereafter. You might already understand firsthand that anxiety is a common occurrence and natural reaction to a trauma-induced event. Even the latest news headlines reporting excessive violence and mayhem can trigger panic and angst.

Take this mindful moment to design your own private safe haven, a shelter of safety and protection from harm.

1.   *Find a calm place to sit and rest. Begin by noticing your breathing.*

2.   *Now imagine yourself in your safe haven. This safe haven can be real or imagined. What would it look like? Pay attention to the details and make a mental or written list of everything it would contain. Perhaps it's modeled after an old-fashioned log cabin with a wood-burning stove and freshly cut flowers on the kitchen table. Perhaps it's tucked away safely in a quiet forest next to a flowing river. Perhaps it's a simple bedroom filled with all the artifacts that are familiar and comforting to you, such as your bed, nightstand, bookshelves, computer, the vase your mother gave you as a*

gift, your favorite painting, photographs of your family and friends, and so on. Perhaps you prefer a resort or fancy hotel in the Caribbean with a luxurious spa and breathtaking view of towering palm trees and sky-blue ocean. Wherever you are, worries and responsibilities are far behind you.

3. *What feelings come up when you imagine this safe spot? Perhaps you are content, unhindered by worry, and contemplative. Perhaps you feel at ease, undisturbed, and peaceful. Take this quiet moment to picture yourself relaxing in your place of safety, experiencing your emotions—some pleasant and some not-so-pleasant—and just settling into it. For a few minutes, you have nowhere to be, nothing to do, and no one depending on you. Just enjoy your tranquil space.*

16.

create your own

Where are your sanctuaries and what are the sources of relaxation and safety in your life now?

Use the space below to create your own meditation or practice for relaxing and feeling safe. Let mindfulness and kindness guide you. Look closely, listen deeply, and trust yourself.

daily meditations for
embracing joys and fears

Today, as I notice different experiences, inside and outside of my body, I will acknowledge the moment consciously, with kindness and compassion, and I will practice establishing and maintaining mindfulness of both joys and fears, in order to see more clearly.

IN THIS SECTION

Being *mindful* means paying attention on purpose with a friendly and curious attitude that does not cling nor seek to make anything change or go away. You establish mindfulness by *intentional attention*. Mindfulness arises from paying attention on purpose with an open heart and an open mind. You can pay attention mindfully to *any* experience. By remembering the focus of your attention when your mind wanders, you can come back to the experience, and to the present moment.

Mindfulness involves attention that is "full," also. Full attention is attention that is interested and inclusive and does not overlook or exclude. Full attention embraces joys and fears, the pleasant and the unpleasant, with curiosity, affection, and compassion. Full attention is also steady and focused. Full attention stays, for the most part, where it is aimed and then comes back as often as necessary, from distraction.

Your ability to focus and maintain attention actually grows with meditation practice. As this concentration of attention grows, awareness strengthens and brightens, much as a brighter flashlight (with a more concentrated beam) enables you to illuminate any shadow more fully. When the object in the shadow is illuminated by more concentrated (stronger) light, then you can see it more clearly and completely.

By paying attention mindfully to both joys and fears—experiences happening inside and outside of your body that are pleasant or unpleasant—you immediately change your relationship to what is happening. In effect, you become far more observant and responsive and less overidentified and unconsciously reactive to whatever may be happening in the moment, and without losing your deep connection with the experience at all.

For example, when you are more mindful while eating, you probably notice an inner feeling of fullness arising well before your plate is actually empty. You probably then stop eating rather than overeat. Overeating is often driven by unconscious habits or in reaction to uncomfortable emotions rather than simply by recognizing and responding to the body's signals of fullness.

An additional benefit of establishing mindfulness in different situations is that you also make a stronger connection with the richness and possibilities that are present. Instead of being lost in memories of the past or in plans for the future or in a thousand other mental reactions, you pay attention, on purpose, to the smell of a flower or to the song of a bird, for example, and thus you open to a much richer experience of the fullness of life within and around you.

And an important benefit of bringing full attention to challenging experiences like anxiety, fear, or panic is that mindful attention reveals that no matter how distressing the experience is, it is *not* you and is *not* permanent. The experience is only an intense energy moving through the present moment.

The meditations and practices in this section are all aimed at helping you experience the naturalness and immediacy of being mindful in a variety of situations. The meditations are also designed to help you embrace all experience by cultivating mindful attention that is strong and steady in the face of either joys or fears.

Some of the meditations are brief and light; others are deeper and point to the power of mindfulness to help you see with clear comprehension into complex experiences and situations. Explore and experiment with the practices in any order you like. Life is waiting for you!

AS YOU PRACTICE

It can be useful to keep some key points in mind as you explore these meditations and practices.

- *Establishing mindfulness is easier than you might think.* You already have what it takes! When establishing mindfulness seems difficult, it is probably because your energy is low, your mind is distracted, or you may be having doubts or a lack of courage to face what is present. Use this insight about energy, distraction, doubt, and courage to look more deeply. Maintain kindness and compassion for yourself; see what you might learn and how you might grow beyond any self-imposed limitations to realize your wholeness and mystery as a human being.

- *In establishing mindfulness, be patient whenever your attention wanders.* Notice frustration in yourself and be kind with it, too.

- *There is more happening than you think!* Full attention means not being blinded or limited by what you think you already know. Stop feeding or fighting any thoughts you have, and let direct experience come to you. In mindfulness practice, we call this "the way of *not*-knowing." It means letting go of what you think you know, good or bad, right or wrong, and being willing to just pay attention on purpose with an open mind and an open heart.

- *In establishing mindfulness, recognizing that conditions are constantly changing is very useful.* Notice any tendency to fight the conditions or the changes and let that go. For example, instead of protesting internally about loud noises when you are trying to meditate, let those noises be and include them with all the other sounds. Or when your thoughts are busy, try just noticing the busyness rather than getting caught up in what the thoughts are actually saying. Treat them as gusts of wind, blowing through your mind.

- *Full attention often leads to unexpected joy and wonder.* Think of the first time you ever tasted an orange.

Or reflect on the wonder in a child's face when they first see the ocean or a snowfall. Experience life's blessings and mystery with curiosity, openness, and affection. Allowing yourself to be surprised by what you notice is a direct benefit of practicing mindfulness. See for yourself.

keep in mind

- The present moment is constantly changing, with joys and fears and pleasant and unpleasant experiences flowing through it.

- As you learn and remember to establish mindfulness through steady and allowing attention in many different situations, your ability to be present and to stay present—regardless of the distractions—will strengthen.

- Your rewards will include a deeper experience of life's richness, and enhanced responsiveness and clarity in everyday activities, including facing and mastering the challenges of fear, panic, and anxiety.

count your breaths: the power to strengthen attention

It is important to discover the power of mindful breathing to help you establish mindfulness and presence in widely different situations. In many cases, more strength (or concentration) of attention is the key to staying present. Use the method in this meditation, counting your breath mindfully, to explore concentrating attention. More concentrated attention steadies your connection to the present moment and overcomes the habits of inattention and easy distractibility.

1. *Sit comfortably in a place where you won't be interrupted.*

2. *Give yourself at least fifteen to twenty minutes for this practice at first, and then vary the length, practicing for briefer periods and longer ones in future sessions.*

3. *Begin breathing mindfully.*

4. *Locate each in breath and out breath and the space between them.*

5. *As you watch and feel your breath mindfully, notice the point where the out breath ends.*

6. *Quietly count each breath at the point it ends, beginning with 1 and going up to 8, for example, "in, out, 1 . . . in, out, 2 . . . in, out, 3," and so on, up to 8.*

   - *If you get to 8, count down in the same way until you get back to 1.*
   - *If you get lost or interrupted, go back to 1.*
   - *Remember to keep your count totally synchronized with the end of the out breath.*

7. Don't worry about how far you count. It is about concentrating attention on the breath, not on how you count!

8. After awhile, drop the count, and just stay on the breath. Remember to relax and allow each breath to come to you.

2.

the tao of anxiety

For many, anxiety is a burdensome and disruptive disorder that makes even the simplest task seem impossible. Take this opportunity to be mindful of what your anxious thoughts are telling you. Worrisome thoughts are a sign or signal; they contain a message for you to decipher that will help guide you to a place of well-being. The following three contemplative questions call to you to understand yourself better and to consider what changes can take place to improve your well-being.

1. *Begin by asking yourself, "What does it mean that I developed an anxiety disorder? What am I supposed to learn from this?" Life is full of challenges and lessons. Some people have to cope with depression or autism or other mental and physical health conditions. Ask yourself, "What can anxiety teach me?" Perhaps you have learned to be more compassionate toward others who suffer with anxiety. Perhaps anxiety introduced you to new emotional depths that have tested your strength and endurance. Perhaps you have learned that despite how overwhelmingly consuming anxiety can be, you have survived every episode and you have succeeded and triumphed many times over. Take this still moment to acknowledge the countless times that you have faced your worst fears,*

fallen down, stood up again, dusted yourself off, and found the strength to move forward.

2. *Next ask yourself, "What are my mind and body trying to reveal to me?" Perhaps you care about self-preservation and self-nurturing. Your anxious thoughts are there because you value being careful, thinking things or actions through cautiously. Your mind and body offer warning signs to help you avoid risky situations. Or maybe your mind and body keep you from having the fun that others have because you cannot free yourself to take the risk. Sit with these contemplations and sift through the ones that apply or resonate with you.*

3. *The last question is most important: "What does your inner wisdom tell you must occur in order for you to recover?" Perhaps you are ready to delve more deeply into understanding the root cause and cure for your anxiety. Perhaps you need to resolve an old wound with family or a loved one. Perhaps you are ready to find new meaning and spiritual guidance in your life. Let your anxiety symptoms help you see what needs to be healed in your life.*

you've got what it takes!

You just got a promotion at work. You should be ecstatic, elated, and filled with pride, but instead you feel riddled with fears and expectations. You may be thinking, "What if I can't make it? What if the work is too demanding? What if I fail? What if their expectations are too high? I'm not sure I can handle this new workload." What should be a time of celebration becomes a time of unrelenting self-doubt. You feel discouraged before you've even headed out of the starting gate.

You have a right to enjoy life's rewards and to acknowledge your accomplishments without having the experience marred by the monster of self-doubt. When anxiety interferes with your self-confidence and tarnishes your sense of competency, try this meditation for reestablishing calm and focus.

1. *Rewind the negative self-talk and just focus on the promotion announcement. What did your boss say? How did he or she say it? Consider your boss's enthusiasm and joy in announcing your promotion after reviewing your excellent work and dedication. Be mindful of your efforts and skills that brought you to this very well-earned moment.*

2. *You are being rewarded for your talent and capabilities. Acknowledge this wholeheartedly by saying aloud or*

internally to yourself, "I am an accomplished person. This promotion reflects my strengths and excellent performance on the job. I am capable of excelling and succeeding. I was offered this promotion because my boss is confident that I am the best person for the position. I have confidence that I will perform my best. And that will be good enough."

3. Even good news can be cause for alarm. But don't let it steal your pleasure. Share your good news with your partner. Send an e-mail to your friends announcing your new promotion. Make dinner reservations at your favorite restaurant and celebrate!

drop in to this moment: tasting the immediacy of mindfulness

Wherever you are, whatever is happening, you can make an immediate shift into greater awareness and clarity with mindfulness. Simply decide to pay attention on purpose without trying to change anything. "Drop in" with friendly and "allowing" attention, and discover what awaits.

1. *Take any comfortable position, including standing.*

2. *Focus attention deliberately in this moment.*

3. *If it helps, quietly repeat a phrase like "Now, this moment" to sharpen attention.*

4. *Bring mindful attention to whatever is in the foreground of your awareness. For example, if a sound is there, just hear it. If there is something you see—color, shape, movement, light, or shadow—notice it. If there is a sensation, smell, or taste in the foreground, notice its texture, intensity, and other qualities directly.*

5. *When thoughts or stories arise in your mind or become distracting, notice them mindfully. Allow them. Name them as "just thoughts." Let them be.*

6. *Throughout this meditation, keep your attention broad and open; let awareness be soft and gentle.*

7. *Let life come to you and flow on—in and out of this moment.*

5.

pamper yourself

Can you remember when your fears and anxiety first erupted in your life? When asked about her earliest recollections of anxiety, a woman I know described being shaped by her parents' fears as a child. Her parents frequently shouted their warnings: "Be careful! Watch out! Don't do that! You'll hurt yourself!" As she grew up, the message that she took into adulthood was that it's a big, scary world out there and you can't trust anyone or anything or you'll be in terrible danger. Fear and worry escalated in every aspect of her life—from getting out of bed every day to the first day of school to going for a job interview. Anxiety, for some, can start as early as childhood.

When you can examine the early markers for anxiety in your life, you can find ways to be more gentle and compassionate with yourself now.

1. *Begin by trying to recollect when your anxious thoughts first began and when they started to negatively influence your life. Perhaps you too were raised in a family that repeatedly warned you against everyday risks and dangers. Or perhaps you were put in a parental position at an early age, forced to care for your siblings before you felt emotionally mature enough to do so. Or perhaps there was a single traumatic*

event that occurred that you never quite got over. Consider what components of your past have played a part in shaping your anxiety and your reactions in life.

2. Now imagine that seated across from you is your nonanxious self, from your earliest memories of who you were, before anxiety became this insurmountable burden. If you were just a small child, then recognize that you are now an adult and have resources at your disposal. You don't have to respond to life the way you did when you were younger. You can learn to care for yourself much as a mother would care for her beloved child.

3. Say aloud or silently to yourself, "I want you to enjoy each and every day. I want you to experience the joys and sorrows in life with equal zest and enthusiasm. The world is full of magnificent beauty and inspiring mystery. Drink it in and celebrate every precious moment of it." Consider what you would say to your own child to encourage her to feel unafraid and open to a world of possibilities. Give yourself the understanding and compassion that you need now.

Remember that with kindness and love toward yourself, you can let go of anxiety and live a full, joyful life, unburdened by the past.

put yourself first

Are you a people pleaser? Do you find yourself with an excessive need for approval? People with anxiety often experience a strong aversion to rejection, so they may overcompensate by trying very hard to make everyone happy, except themselves. You may put undue pressure on yourself to always be polite and happy—never upset or discontented.

You likely believe that your self-worth is directly tied to caring for others. The underlying fear is rejection from others, so you go out of your way to please and accommodate everyone—strangers and loved ones alike—at the expense of yourself.

To take care of everyone else's needs before your own can be exhausting. Over time, resentment and frustration can build up and can result in chronic stress and anxiety. What if a simple daily meditation could help relieve this stress by bringing to light how you can best take care of yourself?

1. *Take this moment to sit in silence. It's just you and your chair and your breath. Don't try to hush the many voices in your head, urging you to "Do this" and "Don't forget that." Just allow these thoughts to swim through your mind and eventually spiral out. They're just your thoughts, worries, to-do lists, and reminders. You can listen to them and sort*

through them later. For now, you are giving yourself permission to be here in this quiet space. You are honoring your right to let the stillness infuse your mind and body.

2. Pay attention to the feelings that arise when you're busy taking care of everyone else. You may feel resentful that others do not consider your feelings and often expect you to do everything. You may feel discouraged that your needs wind up at the bottom of the list.

3. You are an excellent caretaker of others, so let's consider how you can take better care of yourself. Say aloud or internally to yourself, "I am learning to recognize how I put aside my needs in order to take care of others and how this affects me and my anxiety. When I put myself first, I am taking responsibility for caring for myself the very best that I can. When I love myself and acknowledge the importance of my needs, I am putting my needs on an equal footing with the needs of others."

4. When you're ready, get up from your chair and go back into the world, prepared to put yourself first.

7.

I know you, fear: a mindfulness meditation on fear and its associates

Fear is not you and is not permanent, yet it can be intimate, dense, and distracting. In this meditation, which uses the foundation of mindfulness, you can look deeply and clearly at fear and its associates, including anxiety, and the thoughts and bodily sensations that accompany them. Notice how worried thoughts, bodily fear sensations, and feelings of aversion and dislike for the unpleasantness of the fear-filled experience feed and condition each other.

What you learn through clear seeing of the interdependencies between thoughts, body reactions, and aversive feelings can be a powerful step toward healing, transformation, and freedom.

Allow yourself at least fifteen to twenty minutes at first to do this meditation in its entirety. Add more time in later sessions if you wish. You may also wish to come back to this meditation on different occasions over extended periods of time to see what new discoveries you can make with each new investigation into anxious thoughts, fear in your body, and feelings of dislike for the experience.

1. *Find a comfortable place to sit, where you won't be interrupted.*

2. *Let any tightness or contraction in your body soften and relax.*

3. *Breathe mindfully for several minutes, relaxing as you do.*

4. *Gently and deliberately invite a fear or worry to come forward in your thoughts. Soften and relax as you turn toward the fearful thought and let yourself hear it.*

5. *Open your focus and notice any place in your body that is reacting to the fearful thoughts. Breathe mindfully and let those places in the body soften and relax as much as they can.*

6. *Take time and find the space around the fear or worry in your body. This may be as easy as widening the focus and sensing other sensations nearby. Notice the place where the sense of holding or contracting begins to fade or is not present. Breathe mindfully for a few more breaths if that helps you steady and calm your attention. Notice how the body is interconnected with the worried thoughts and feeds on them.*

7. *Now, let your body rest and shift attention back to your thoughts. Breathe mindfully.*

8. *Just listen to the thoughts. You don't have to fight, argue, deny, or feed the thoughts. Just notice them, letting them come and go. From time to time, remind yourself, "They are only*

thoughts and stories." Notice the "tone of your mind's voice." Notice the space between the thoughts. What do the thoughts say? Let them speak without arguing back.

9. Remember to breathe mindfully for a few breaths from time to time, coming back, feeling the breath sensations, and resting there. Also notice and allow any body reactions to move and settle, as much as they can.

10. Now, shift attention from thoughts or sensations to any feelings of dislike, hatred, or aversion you notice toward the experience of fear or worry or toward your body's reactions. Such feelings are usually the product of the feeling of unpleasantness associated with the fearful thoughts or with the body's fear reactions.

11. Look more deeply at the energies of dislike, hatred, and aversion. Have they spawned thoughts and bodily reactions of their own? Let yourself soften and release as much as possible when you notice any contraction in your body.

12. Keep breathing mindfully, noticing thoughts and sensations, relaxing, observing, and allowing the patterns of fear and its reactions to flow and be seen without fighting or feeding them.

13. Pay particular attention to any angry or mean thoughts that may be arising, for example, "I hate this feeling," "I wish it would go away," "I must be crazy," "I am doomed," or "Something bad is wrong with me." Breathe mindfully and hear them, without feeding or fighting them.

14. *From time to time as you notice such mean and critical thinking, gently remind yourself, "I am not my thoughts," "They are only thoughts," or "I don't have to fight them or feed them any more." Breathe mindfully and let your body soften and relax. Rest in the open spaces in your body around any areas of contraction.*

15. *Continue noticing thoughts, feelings, and bodily reactions. See how they often seem to feed each other. Notice the power of dislike and aversion for the experience and how that aversion affects the present moment.*

16. *Continue being mindful as each element of the fear experience reveals itself. Trust yourself to rest in spaciousness and steady attention no matter how frightening or demanding thoughts, feelings, and sensations may seem.*

17. *Notice how all the elements change as you watch them. What was so loud moments ago is not even here now. Sensations, thoughts, aversion—they all come and go.*

18. *End by offering kindness and compassion to yourself and to all of your experiences, even the unpleasant ones. If it helps, picture a healing white light surrounding you as you breathe in and out mindfully. Let yourself bathe in the light and relax.*

19. *When you are finished, reflect on your experience. What have you discovered about yourself and the patterns and habits of fear?*

8.

dissolve it away

Anxiety can often feel like a suffocating spandex bodysuit that makes you sweat negative thoughts from head to toe. It can make you feel like you're trapped in that sticky body armor for eternity. Let's try a meditation for dissolving the armor of anxiety and freeing up your mind and body to experience the beauty that awaits you.

1. *First, take notice of just how clingy and cumbersome your outfit feels against your skin. It must feel uncomfortable to move, stretch, or change positions. Ensnared in your doubts and fears, you may feel depressed, isolated, and even angry. When you're fastened inside the spandex suit, it has a vise grip on your emotional stability. You can hardly get out of bed to get your life started.*

2. *Now close your eyes and visualize your body armor dissolving. Start with your head, face, and neck. The spandex is melting and disappearing, clearing your senses—sight, hearing, smell, and touch. Move downward toward your shoulders, arms, hands, fingers, and chest. The elastic is vaporizing into thin air, letting you open your lungs and breathe more freely. Move downward to your belly, back, and waist. Your suit is peeling away more and more, loosening*

the grip of your fears and doubts on your life. Descend to your hips, buttocks, and legs. You can hardly feel the outline of that clinging armor of negativity. Drop down to your ankles, feet, and toes. The dark, tumultuous thoughts are evaporating, leaving you weightless and free.

3. *At last, the depressing thoughts that were once stealing your clarity and freedom are vanishing into nothingness.*

4. *Without the spandex outfit, you can feel the light breeze on your skin, you can see how the sunlight disperses through the curtains, you can smell the jasmine wafting from a nearby garden, you can hear the far-off hum of the music of life. You are no longer trapped or constricted. You're free to move and breathe on your own.*

9.

wanted: compassion

Meditation offers a unique opportunity to cultivate emotional balance and promote positive states of mind, such as compassion. Compassion is a powerful key to unlocking empathy, generosity, and love. Compassion allows you to feel a shared sense of suffering along with a heartfelt desire for others to be free from pain or suffering. This next meditation will enhance your compassion as a coping tool to overcome the more stressful emotions.

1. *Get seated, relax your limbs, and close your eyes. Pay attention to the weight of your eyelids and the restful sensation migrating into your arms and legs. Each in breath invigorates and brings life to each and every part of your body. Each out breath calms and restores tranquility to your mind and spirit.*

2. *Consider what compassion means to you. What does it feel like? When did you express it last? When did you receive it from someone else? Perhaps you experienced empathy when you saw a woman trying desperately to console her crying baby. Perhaps you felt compassion toward a homeless person on the way to work this morning. Perhaps a stranger acknowledged you struggling with an emotional meltdown*

and offered a kind word or smile that lightened your heavy feelings for a brief reprieve.

3. *Now select a specific compassionate memory and delve further into it. Scan your experience for feelings, thoughts, sensations, and reactions. Imagine your enormous capacity to extend compassion to yourself the next time you feel anxious.*

4. *Think back on a time when someone showed you compassion. Perhaps a close friend expressed tenderness and understanding when you were going through a difficult time and was able to shoulder some of your emotional burden. Visualize this compassion being offered by others as if it were a constant flow of energy during times of fear, worry, or panic. Reflect on this story of kindness throughout your day to keep stressful thoughts from inhibiting your vital connection to joy.*

10.

walking mindfully: reconnecting with the present moment through movement

This meditation for mindfully walking may seem odd at first, but you will be rewarded for your efforts at practicing it.

Walking mindfully can be especially helpful in times when you are feeling agitated, confused, or "spaced out." You can practice this meditation for brief periods or explore it over longer sessions of up to thirty or even forty-five minutes or more. This meditation can also be done in small spaces— an office with the door closed or a bedroom, for example. It is also very nice when done outside in nature.

1. *Identify a path to walk on, perhaps as long as fifteen or twenty paces, but it could be less.*

2. *Standing still, bring mindful attention to your body and to the sensations of standing. Notice heaviness, air on skin, sensations in feet, legs, hands, arms, back, shoulders, head, and face.*

3. *When you feel the intention to move, take your first step. Notice which foot starts, how weight shifts, the feeling of*

pushing and lifting the foot, and how it swings forward with the stepping. Notice the movement of the foot going down after it steps forward and how it lands on the ground.

4. In doing this meditation, it is helpful to walk quite slowly at first and to take short steps of about the length of your foot. This will help your balance.

5. Notice how sensations in one foot fade and are replaced by sensations arising in the other foot as that one begins its step.

6. When your attention moves to something else besides walking, patiently and gently notice it. Let it be. You have not done anything wrong. It is only your mind moving and doing what all minds do. Kindly bring attention back to your feet and the walking.

7. Walk mindfully to the end of your path. When you get to the end, stop. Feeling the momentum of walking fade and the sensations of the stopped body arise, relax. Notice your breath. Notice other experiences.

8. Notice the intention to turn and to begin walking again when it arises. If you like, follow that intention. Walk mindfully back down your path.

9. Continue walking mindfully as long as you like. What do you notice when your walking period ends? What do you notice next?

center of attention

Some social situations are easier than others. You may feel completely at ease around your family, friends, and coworkers—people you know well and who know and accept you. But still there are a number of occasions when a particular social norm, such as being teased or criticized in public, can trigger your anxiety. Rationally, you know that it's just a normal part of social interactions. People poke fun at each other all the time—everyone laughs at themselves.

Where things get stressful and uncomfortable for you is when you're the center of attention—all eyes are on you, all laughter is about you, all of the focus is centered around your mistake. What do you do? Where can you turn to avoid further embarrassment? The good news is that the awkward moment won't last long; a new conversation quickly diverts attention away from you and onto the next topic at hand.

The next time you're feeling like the butt of the joke or scrutinized in front of others, the following exercise may bring you some relief.

1. *For times when stepping away would simply be impossible without drawing further attention to yourself, practice the art of acceptance. Acceptance represents nonresistance—a*

willingness to not fight it or back away but to just let things be as they are.

2. *Be gentle with yourself and your emotional reactions. You may be feeling overly sensitive or unable to laugh alongside others. You may feel defensive and fearful of rejection. Take a moment to focus on your breath and allow each in breath to fill your body with self-acceptance for what you cannot change and allow each out breath to release the tension and stress from deep within.*

3. *Say inwardly, "I can let this go. I am willing to take life as it comes. Soon this will pass and calmness will be restored."*

When you can relax and tolerate life's imperfections and mishaps, you can learn to laugh at yourself. It makes your journey through life a whole lot lighter.

12.

send goodwill

As your daily workload skyrockets and work pressures mount, you may sometimes feel frustrated, irritated, angry, or defeated. At times you may even wonder if your coworkers don't care, notice, or want to help you. It may feel like you're facing it all alone and that no one cares if you sink or swim. Your situation may seem chaotic and out of control, which can lead to anxiety. Frustration and exhaustion can lead to negative thought cycles.

Take this moment to reduce work-related tension and embrace kindness and hope by sending goodwill to one and all. Here's how you do that:

1. *Start with yourself. Sit quietly and focus on breathing deeply from the abdomen at first, and then pay attention to how your breathing gets slower and slower.*

2. *Now take another slow, gradual, methodical in breath and on your out breath, visualize this breath of life filled whole-heartedly with the intention of goodwill toward yourself and others. Each out breath represents the positive potential for magnificent growth combined with a feeling of tranquility and loving-kindness to every coworker.*

3. *When a difficult occasion arises at work or someone at work is not being helpful, take a few minutes to send this person an exhalation of goodwill. During times of conflict and inflated negative ruminations, remember to send kindness inward and outward. It takes practice but it will reduce negative interactions and allow benevolence and positive energy to circulate more generously within and all around you. And, as an added bonus, it'll help you feel less anxious.*

your inner body: a mindfulness meditation for connecting directly with your body

Stress and the body's reaction to it can be a trigger for anxiety and worry. Unmanaged chronic stress, with its physical tensions and distress, can also be a maintaining factor in chronic anxiety.

By developing your ability to quickly connect with the "inner landscape" of your body, revealed in direct experience of changing physical sensations, moment by moment, you can help your mind and body relax and ease the effects of anxiety and fear. Strengthen your conscious connection with your body by practicing this meditation both formally and as deeply and for as long as you like. Practice informally by "tuning in" to your direct physical experience for a few breaths throughout the day. Let wisdom from each practice direct you in wise self-care.

1. *Take a comfortable position, with your body well-supported and relaxed.*

2. *Let go of any agenda or requirements for changing anything.*

3. Put attention on your breath and breathe mindfully for a few minutes. Close your eyes if that helps.

4. Let your attention be curious, gentle, friendly, and allowing.

5. When you like, softly expand your focus to also include all the other direct physical sensations flowing through your body, as they reveal themselves, in this moment.

6. Let the sensations come to you, not pulling or pushing any of them, just letting them be as they are.

7. Let each sensation move at its own speed through the body region and through your awareness.

8. Notice the strongest sensations first, then, as attention becomes more sensitive, notice more and more subtle ones, all moving, all changing.

9. Notice the sensations directly, feeling vibration, pressure, contraction, expansion, heaviness, and so on. Don't get caught in ideas or stories about what the sensations mean. Just allow your attention to rest in different places, parts, and regions of your body, feeling the sensations happening there directly.

10. Notice the aliveness of your body as sensations pulse through each region or part.

11. If you wish, acknowledge gratitude and appreciation to your body for carrying you through this life.

12. Practice for as long as you like. End by opening your eyes and moving gently.

cultivate patience

Life gets messy, complicated, and full of disorder and ambiguity. You may find that difficult situations cannot be worked out immediately and require time, patience, and an ability to wait for the solution to unfold gradually. You may not always be able to resolve things quickly or know in advance how something is going to work out. You can make yourself feel extremely anxious at such times when things don't work out as planned.

Cultivating patience involves being tolerant of life's temporary, unsolved predicaments and uncertainties while you wait for a solution or opportunity to emerge. Patience requires trust. You nurture your ability to trust that the natural flow of life has moments that cannot be controlled or easily fixed. Life has an uncanny way of working itself out, with or without you.

1. *Give yourself permission to walk away from the situation. Literally, you may want to take a walk or leave the room. Fight the urge to go back in and haggle over the solution. Just remove yourself from the troublesome area.*

2. *Once you've taken a time-out, check in with yourself. How's your breathing? Are you hungry, thirsty, or tired? When was the last time you took a break and stretched your body?*

3. *Affirmations can help develop an attitude of patience and trust. Try these or make up your own: "Patience starts with me. When I practice patience, I am allowing myself to accept the things in life that are ambiguous, uncertain, and undefined. When I stop micromanaging every step along the way, I am widening my perspective and trusting that problems in life eventually resolve themselves." Write these affirmations down and post them up at work as daily reminders of your ability to stay calm and be patient.*

Over time, as you cultivate patience and trust within yourself, you'll learn to relax and tolerate life's unpredictable moments. You'll learn to let go and wait for the answer or solution to surface in its own time.

15.

but what do I say?

Social gatherings can be frightening places, triggering anxiety like fireworks in your stomach. One friend described a time when he drove to a party, parked, and sat in his car agonizing about how he might not know a single person—except the host. After about five minutes, he drove back home. He simply couldn't endure the pressure of feeling insecure and out of place in a social situation.

If this is familiar to you, you may feel like you don't know what to say, how to make small talk, or how to act around strangers without coming off as shy, on edge, and nervous. The following exercise can be employed before, during, or after a social gathering and will help you close the distance that you put between yourself and other people, especially in groups.

1. *Find a place to sit or stand while you reconnect with the part of yourself that would truly like to attend the gathering, be social, meet people, and have a good time. Deep down, each of us wants to have fun and enjoy the company of others, even strangers.*

2. *Recognize the negative self-talk that is simultaneously going on. What kind of things are you saying to yourself about attending?*

- *"I don't know what to say to other people."*

- *"What if I say the wrong thing?"*

- *"What if other people can sense how terrified and nervous I am?"*

- *"I feel uncomfortable with small talk and even moments of silence."*

- *"What if no one likes me or if I come across as an introvert?"*

- *"What if I embarrass myself?"*

3. *Recall an occasion when you were recently able to start or maintain a conversation with someone. Pay attention to the way you held yourself and your ability to listen, make eye contact, ask questions, and disclose something about yourself. Perhaps it was with your boss, coworker, friend, neighbor, or therapist. In that precise moment, you had confidence and self-worth. Someone listened to you and you listened to him.*

4. *Take this quiet reprieve to acknowledge that you are unique and interesting just the way you are. Avoid berating or punishing yourself or telling yourself you should be something that you're not. As you discover the courage to be your true self, remember that when you love yourself, love and beauty emanate outward. As you accept yourself, whether you feel particularly shy or inward or tongue-tied, you are allowing others to accept you as well. In fact, you are radiating acceptance for each and every person around you such that they can just be themselves too.*

16.

create your own

Where and when in the flow of your daily life would you like to feel more connected and present?

Use the space below to create your own meditation or practice for establishing mindfulness and presence. Let mindfulness and kindness guide you. Look closely, listen deeply, and trust yourself.

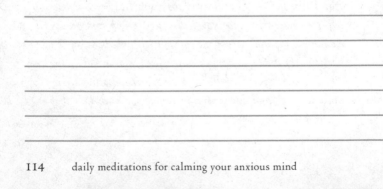

daily meditations for
befriending your anxious
mind and body

*Today, as challenging experiences and intense energies arise,
either outside or inside of me, I will notice how I tend to
treat them and practice intentionally nurturing kindness and
compassion toward myself and the world around me.*

IN THIS SECTION

The meditations and practices in this section are focused on
one thing: how are you treating life? (Rather than the usual
question, how is life treating you?)

Are you fighting life, condemning it, ignoring it, liking it,
wanting it, or what? "Life" here means the living things and
situations of this world in and around you. "Life" includes
especially *yourself* and all your parts and pieces (and *not* forget-
ting the unpleasant ones, like anxiety, fear, and pain). The
"life" that is here and happening right now, in this moment,
is the subject, because life happens only now, in the present
moment.

What if you actually made a commitment to more friendliness, being more welcoming, and to cherishing life, at least
for the time it takes to do a meditation practice? What if you
decided—for even a few mindful breaths—*not* to put anyone
or anything out of your heart, no matter what their state of
mind or behavior (understanding that you do not have to
approve or encourage their behavior as a condition of keeping
them "in your heart")?

Many meditation teachers have pointed out that mindfulness is a way of paying attention that contains kindness and compassion for whatever is present. Yet unconscious habits of judging and criticizing are not kind or compassionate. They can distort and obscure the clarity of mindfulness and the benefits that follow from clear seeing in the present moment. And habits of self-criticism and judgment, when ignored or unconscious, can actually be maintaining factors, if not triggers, for anxiety and worry.

If you could practice cherishing more and not closing your heart so much by old habits of criticism and condemnation of yourself or others, or rejection of the experience unfolding here in the present moment, what might you learn? How might your own life unfold differently, beginning now?

What if you discovered you had within you a greatness of heart unsuspected? What if you found that peace was closer than you thought because it is *you* who has the power to abandon the fight? What if you started with cherishing and soothing yourself and the contents of your inner life? What if you could make peace with any feelings of vulnerability and limitation within you, as they arise and are felt?

The meditations and practices in this section invite you to approach life with exactly these questions in mind. They all begin with a perspective that kindness and compassion can be deliberately practiced. These meditations offer various approaches, images, and skills to meet situations and conditions of daily life and inner life, not with judgment and dislike, but intentionally, with friendliness and welcome.

As your understanding deepens as to the force or "power" of kindness and compassion as actual practices you can do, you will likely find that the light of your mindfulness grows much brighter as well.

Unpleasant conditions or situations (like feelings of fear, panic, anxiety, or pain) evoke a tendency in us to want to be rid of them and to dislike or even to make war on them in the effort to drive them away. The ironic truth is, however, that the harder we tend to fight something like fear or pain, the stronger it seems to get! The reactive, habitual action toward such unpleasantness is to make war on it. But how successful is that, in your experience? Can you really make war on fear—or on anxiety, worry, or pain—and win?

Habits of disliking and pushing away, making war, and fighting the threatening or the unpleasant are very deep. Rather than following those patterns unconsciously, use these meditations to explore the territory of befriending mind and body. Since kindness and compassion are already in you, it could be easier than you think to practice them as meditations and intentional actions!

AS YOU PRACTICE

Recalling some basic points about practicing kindness and compassion as meditations can help as you investigate this section.

- *You do not have to "imagine" anything.* Kindness and compassion are already in you. In some sense, the meditations and practices in this section are simply pointing you toward those qualities already existing inside you and inviting you to explore them, seeing how they flow or are blocked during your encounter with life, moment by moment.

- *A key to practicing kindness and friendliness lies in recognizing when you are not feeling those things!* When you notice that, pay closer attention to what keeps the mean feelings going. See where and how you can stop feeding them, how you can abandon them without making more hate or war on them! Sometimes it can be as simple as noticing you are trying to make something go away and just stopping that attempt, just letting it be.

- *When you do a loving-kindness meditation, actively wishing yourself or another happiness or well-being, it is okay to feel whatever arises in you.* You do *not* have to feel happy or loving, especially at first. And if sad or angry feelings arise in you, they are okay too. They probably reflect some long-ignored pain within you that feels safe enough at last to come forward. Remember to meet whatever comes forward with welcome and compassion.

keep in mind

- Mindfulness has a welcoming and friendly quality to it.

- By recognizing deep habits of meanness and war-making within, you can free yourself to be more present and to know more accurately, and to respond more wisely, to what is here, now.

- You can strengthen the qualities of kindness and compassion through explicit meditation and practice and with a commitment to pay attention to how you are treating the world rather than be blocked by a story about how the world is treating you.

stopping the war: on not hating your upset feelings or yourself for having those feelings

From modern psychology we learn that a hostile or fearful thought alone can trigger the body's fight-or-flight reaction, and ancient wisdom teaches that war doesn't end by war, but by love alone. From either of these perspectives, being angry with upset feelings, or with yourself for having them, makes no sense.

Use this meditation to explore taking a different approach to your relationship to your upset feelings.

1. *When you are feeling upset—from anger, fear, or worry, for example—immediately name the upset and make an intention to work with it differently.*

2. *Breathe mindfully for several breaths until you feel more steady and focused.*

3. *Turn mindful attention to your body, feeling the places where the upset is taking the form of sensations.*

4. *Allow the sensations of upset to be, letting yourself soften and open, feeling them and finding the space around them. Notice the larger space beyond the contractions of upset. This larger space actually is capable of containing all the upset.*

5. *Notice any angry thoughts or judgments against yourself or the upset and stop feeding or fighting them. Let them go.*

6. *Rest in your feelings of inner spaciousness and wholeness, breathing mindfully as you practice this meditation. These feelings will not fail you.*

the belly relaxer

When acute stress and excessive worry hold you hostage, do you ever feel your stomach is filled with knots, tightening and clenching with each passing thought? The stomach is a repository for bundled tension that can be hard to shake off. When the belly aches, it's a signal that it needs your attention.

The following exercise will teach you how to pay attention to the tension in your belly and how to reduce stress before it lodges itself in your body.

1. *Find a place to sit or lie down and rest your eyes. Focus on your breathing and the rise and fall of your chest.*

2. *Gently place both hands, palms down, on your belly. Practice breathing from your abdomen, noticing how the belly inflates and deflates with each breath.*

3. *Move your hands slowly in a circular motion on the surface of your belly. Be aware of where your bundles of knots are stored and concentrate this gentle movement in those areas of tension. Do you feel extra tightening just under your rib cage? Or is it lower down, toward your navel? Does your anxiety feel like several boxers pounding away at a punching*

bag? Or does it feel like everything is just clenched down solid like a brick?

4. Continue rubbing your belly and imagine tiny little fists clenching and releasing, opening and closing. You are retraining your mind and body to relax the fists so they can let go of their struggle. Meditate on loosening the grip that stress has on you by visualizing each clenched area as a wide and open palm.

5. Speak your intentions aloud or silently: "I am mindful that I store tension in my belly. I am encircling my clamped muscles with affection and tenderness. I am massaging compassion and mercy into my body, enabling me to release and relax."

When you're ready, begin to move your body and return to your activity at hand, feeling calmer and less tense.

caregiver for yourself

There are mounting demands at work, unrelenting pressures at home, and now you feel like you might be coming down with a cold. It's enough to send you into a state of despair. When you've been taking care of everyone else's needs at the expense of your own, you may be feeling irritable and easily annoyed. You may be experiencing muscle tension or a headache may be forming. How are you going to put aside time just for you? What can you do to take better care of yourself? You need a personalized formula for self-care in order to reprioritize your needs.

- Begin by drawing your attention away from work, home, family, and others, and shifting toward you. Ask yourself this: "What's going on in my body? What is my body telling me? What am I feeling? How can I be more in tune with what my body needs?"

- Consider what your self-care list might consist of. Your health and well-being may be dependent on several key factors:

  1. *Nutrition*
  2. *Exercise*

3. *Stress reduction*

4. *Relationships*

- By examining your relationship to these four pillars of health, you can get a better sense of what you might need right now.

- Take this moment to check in with your core needs by using these four keys to health to identify areas of neglect. You might find the solutions to what ails you. Here are some examples:

  1. *Nutrition:* "I forgot to eat breakfast and now I'm starving and agitated. Time to eat!"

  2. *Exercise:* "This blinding tension in my back usually feels better after I take a brisk walk or jog."

  3. *Stress reduction:* "I didn't sleep at all last night; a quick power nap would restore my energy."

  4. *Relationships:* "I snapped at my partner this morning because I was stressed about running late for work; maybe it's time to call and apologize."

- Make a mental or written list of what you can do to make sure that you take care of your basic needs. Eat, sleep, play, love, and invite wellness into your life every day.

reflection on self-worth

Unconscious habits of self-criticism can undermine your sense of well-being and contribute to anxiety. Use the following meditation to free yourself from self-doubt and self-criticism.

1. *Sit or lie down where you will not be interrupted, and make yourself comfortable.*

2. *Breathe mindfully for a few breaths, letting your mind and body relax and settle.*

3. *Let your attention become increasingly kind and sensitive.*

4. *No need to hurry or rush or to make anything happen. Relax.*

5. *When you feel quiet and ready inside, deliberately pose a question about self-worth, for example, "Do I trust myself?" "Am I strong enough?" "Am I good enough?"*

6. *Drop your question into your heart and mind, like a pebble tossed into a still pond.*

7. *Breathe mindfully, resting in gentle attention and soft awareness.*

8. *Listen for the ripples that come back to you from the question you dropped into the pond. Without judgment or debate, simply listen and allow all the responses that reveal themselves.*

9. *Let mindful breathing and listening hold you and support you.*

10. *Meet any feelings of self-doubt with compassion and kindness.*

11. *Offer them healing and mercy.*

12. *Let wisdom from this reflection guide you.*

follow your heart

An elderly friend of mine who suffers from anxiety often complains that certain situations will cause her heart to practically beat out of her chest. She also experiences excessive sweating, nausea, and trembling in her body. She's been on an anxiety medication for most of her adult life.

It's no picnic in the park when you're in the midst of a full-blown panic attack. The sheer terror of your frantically beating heart is enough to convince you that something is seriously wrong.

This next exercise is about listening to your heart. Your mind might tell you one thing, but what does your heart tell you?

1. *Get yourself in a relaxed position, seated or lying down, and rest your eyes. Let your arms, legs, and body go limp.*

2. *Focus your attention on your heart and notice what's going on. Is it pounding away like a jackhammer? Or is it beating with an unsteady, irregular rhythm? Whatever your heart is doing, take a moment to notice what it might be communicating to you.*

3. *If your heart could speak, what might it be saying to you? "I'm really stressed out right now. Please pay attention to me. Please help me. I need some nurturing right now. I'm scared and I need to know you care about me." Consider the voice of your heart and open yourself to being a good listener.*

4. *Now reflect on ways that you can be more sensitive and caring to the needs of your heart. She's poured out her feelings and vulnerabilities to you. Can you offer her compassion and reassurance that you care?*

When you listen to the language of your heart, you become more proficient at looking after yourself and calming yourself in the heat of the moment.

walk out of the fog

Do you have difficulty concentrating when you're under pressure? You start to get some clarity for a brief moment, and then it evaporates. The simplest task can seem insurmountable, time-consuming, and overwhelmingly complicated. You may experience a brain fog, become easily distracted, and feel unable to pay attention to any single thought. It can be exhausting!

A little boost of physical activity can increase your blood flow, reduce tension, and put you back in your body with more stamina. The anxiety-reducing effects of regular exercise have been well documented.

Consider your favorite ways to get your body moving, such as tennis, jogging, racquetball, free weights, hiking, swimming, and so on. If you're someone who doesn't have a regular exercise program, consider walking in your neighborhood—whatever it takes to get you off the couch, out of your troubles, and into your body.

Test this walking meditation for starters.

1. *Before you start your walk, make sure you've got good walking shoes for arch support, comfort, and shock absorbency. Feel free to warm up by stretching out your calves and leg muscles.*

2. *As you head out the door, take five to ten deep breaths. You're sending a message to all of your cells to wake up and be prepared to move.*

3. *On your walk, be aware of your posture. Walk with an erect spine, your chest stretching wide to let the fresh air in. Let your arms swing opposite the stride of your legs to engage your left and right brain hemispheres.*

4. *Notice any areas of discomfort. Are you out of shape? You might experience some subtle aches and pains initially, but they will ease as you continue this practice and increase your strength and endurance over time.*

Physical exercise should be fun and stimulating. Keep up a daily walking program that consists of twenty to thirty minutes per day. It may be your best defense during times of stress and a quick relief for brain fog.

7.

kind wishes: a basic
loving-kindness meditation

There are a wide variety of meditation methods for practicing and strengthening feelings of kindness and compassion. This particular method, using specific phrases of friendliness and well-wishing, is based on perhaps the most ancient form for practicing loving-kindness meditation known. It is said to have been taught by the Buddha to his followers.

You certainly don't have to be a Buddhist to do this practice. And doing it won't make you a Buddhist! In fact, as you do this meditation, you will probably realize that you actually have done something like it quite often in your life.

The phrase-based method of this practice offers you a specific meditation form that is easy to use and also quite flexible and powerful as a vehicle of healing and transformation in many different situations.

The phrase you select should resonate warmly in your heart. Your wish should be something that any living beings would appreciate, regardless of their material circumstances.

When doing this (or any other loving-kindness or compassion meditation), it is no problem if painful or disturbing feelings or memories arise. Use such feelings as objects for more kind and compassionate attention rather than putting them out of your heart.

You can practice this meditation formally or informally and as long and as often as you like. You can practice with only yourself as an object or with any or all others you wish.

1. *Take a comfortable position, including lying down, if you wish. If it helps, close your eyes.*

2. *Put your attention on your breath and breathe mindfully for a few moments.*

3. *Shift attention to your heart space, in the center of your chest, and notice any feelings or sensations you have there. Let them be, kindly accepting whatever you notice.*

4. *Allow yourself to open and accept feelings of friendliness and kindness that are within you. If it helps, recall a dear friend or loved one or a pet or the warm feeling you have when a child takes your hand. Let the kind feelings arising from these remembrances fill and support you as much as possible.*

5. *Now imagine focusing attention on yourself. Imagine you are speaking to yourself or to a part of yourself that is upset, injured, or needing attention. Speak kindly and with compassion, wishing yourself well. You might use phrases like "May I be safe and peaceful," "May I be happy," "May I be healthy and well," or "May I live with ease and in peace."*

6. *Repeat your phrase or phrases as if you were quietly humming a lullaby to yourself.*

7. *When your attention shifts or other feelings arise, you have not made a mistake. Just notice the shifts and feelings, allow and release them, and return attention to your phrase.*

8. *When you like, if you like, you can shift attention from yourself to a friend or loved one. Imagine speaking kindly and directly to them, wishing them well, using your phrase or phrases.*

9. *If you wish, after a time, shift again. Include others. You could even include groups of friends or loved ones if you wish. Keep your practice simple. Don't get too analytical.*

10. *When you like, you can shift away from friends or loved ones and send kind wishes to strangers, including those far away.*

11. *When you feel ready, try sending kind wishes to someone who causes tension or difficulty for you, even to someone you don't like. Remember, you are not suddenly approving of their hurtful behaviors, but you are practicing looking more deeply and are wishing even these people relief and ease. What does it take to wish these people peace and ease?*

12. *Whenever you need to steady yourself or stabilize your attention, breathe mindfully for a few breaths before resuming your phrase.*

13. You can even send kind wishes to animals or any other living thing you choose.

14. Practice for as long as you like. End your meditation by releasing your phrase and opening your eyes.

break for kindness

General anxiety can manifest in the body in a number of physical ways—hot flashes, excessive sweating, heart palpitations, or feeling sick to your stomach. When this occurs, it can compound your stress levels. It's particularly frustrating when it happens around other people, such as coworkers, colleagues, or students. The last thing you want to do is draw more attention to yourself. The next time your body hits its stress capacity, try this exercise.

1. *You can sit or stand for this one.*

2. *Rather than struggling to ignore or push away our worrisome thoughts, take this moment to reflect on what is bothering you. What is causing your anxiety in this instance? Are you concerned about something at work, home, school, or elsewhere? Are you troubled about the assignment that you're working on? Are you anxious about your children, partner, mother, or someone else's safety? Are you feeling frantic about failure or making a mistake? Check in with your emotions and get to the source of what is prompting your fears to take over.*

3. *Ask yourself this: "What kind of tenderness can I give myself that will help ease my suffering? How can I be more gentle and sensitive with myself now or in the not-so-distant future?" Perhaps you need a nap or a snack or a break to go for a walk. Perhaps you would like to make a call to check in with family or loved ones. Perhaps you just need a hug. You can learn to be kind to yourself when you're stressed and anxious.*

9.

waves of relaxation

You've been tossing and turning all night long with both-
ersome ruminations, and it seems impossible to fall asleep.
"What if I fail the exam tomorrow?" "What if I get sick before
my upcoming vacation?" "I've got to remember to include that
statistic in my report for work." "I'm worried about this hor-
rible news article." And on and on it goes, without an exit
strategy or rest stop for the weary. You're even agonizing over
how tired and spaced out you'll feel tomorrow and how that
will affect your work, performance, attitude, and mood.

Insomnia is a common symptom for anxiety sufferers,
and it can have negative consequences that last for days after-
ward. The following progressive relaxation technique will help
your mind and body secure a place of calm and quiet for the
rest of the night.

1.   *To begin, take several deep breaths and on each out breath, let
     go of your accumulated negative ponderings and the tension
     stored up in your mind and body. Breathe in the serenity.
     Breathe out the anxiety. Try this for several minutes.*

2.   *While lying flat on your back, your body limp and comfort-
     able, rest your arms at your sides with your legs outstretched.
     Start by curling your toes in toward the soles of your feet,*

tightening the muscles for just a second and then releasing. Do this a few times—tighten and then relax, tighten and then relax.

3. *Moving up the body, tighten the muscles in your shins by gently pulling your toes toward you and then release. Two to three times is enough—pull, hold for a second, and then release.*

4. *Now focus on your thighs. Clench the muscles in your thighs, hold momentarily, and then let go. Do this a few times.*

5. *Check in with your breathing. It's important to not hold your breath.*

6. *Move on up to your buttocks. Tighten by pulling them together and then relaxing, tighten and then relax. Notice how your hips and pelvis are beginning to loosen up and go limp.*

7. *Continue this same pattern of tightening and releasing for your stomach, chest, shoulders, arms, hands, neck, jaw, eyes, forehead, and mouth. Remember to keep breathing.*

8. *Scan your body for any residual areas of tension and repeat the tighten-release technique for those muscles.*

9. *Visualize waves of relaxation undulating throughout your body, saturating every muscle and nerve ending, starting at your toes and working their way up to your head.*

When you're done, bask in the relaxation and let yourself drift off to sleep.

10.

self-compassion in
times of upset

A wise relationship to pain and distress begins with compassion for yourself as you bear the burden of pain and distress—either inner or outer—in your own life.

Unfortunately, it is a common reaction to be angry and mean toward pain and upset in yourself, and at times, in others. Very commonly, feelings of fear and vulnerability that lie beneath the immediate pain fuel the energies of anger and hostility that arise toward pain, including pain in yourself.

Compassion offers a way of being in a different relationship with pain. It means literally "together with suffering." Compassion contains both the intent to stay present to the pain and to act to relieve the pain. Staying present, remaining conscious, and acting wisely takes courage, and it is empowering. Compassionate action offers a way of meeting pain that also includes holding any feelings of fear and vulnerability as equally worthy of attention and care.

Use the following meditation to stay present for yourself (and others) and to act compassionately in times of pain and upset, including times of anxiety and fear. Let this meditation support you as a formal practice, and informally, in challenging moments.

1. *When you feel upset or distress from either physical or emotional pain, deliberately bring attention to your body and breath, and begin breathing mindfully.*

2. *As you begin feeling steadier and more focused, open more to the upsetting experiences present in mind and body. Name the upset gently and with compassion—for example, "This is my anxiety about my health," "This is my back pain," "This is my fear about losing my loved one."*

3. *When you notice and name the physical or emotional element of the upset, you could add, "This is how pain, fear, worry, or anger lives and expresses itself in my mind and body."*

4. *Breathe mindfully to remain steady and present for the unfolding experience you are observing in your mind and body. Let yourself relax, soften, and stay open to the experience as best you can.*

5. *Now imagine speaking to and interacting directly with the part or parts of you that are in distress. Kindly offer them relief. Visualize offering a drink of cool water to hot anger. Imagine a gentle touch and massage at the site of pain. Feel yourself making space for anxiety and extending to it a chair or pillow.*

6. *Speak quietly, kindly, and soothingly to the upset: "May you be at peace," "May you be safe," "May you be released."*

7. *Practice as long as you like. Be patient, not requiring any-thing to change. Let your heart fill with compassion and well-wishing for the upset, regardless of what happens next.*

8. *Finish your meditation by speaking compassionately and kindly to yourself—for example, "May I live with peace and ease," "May I be free from fear and pain."*

let the good outweigh the bad

Do you embarrass easily? Do you blush frequently and find yourself explaining to others why your face is glowing red, flushed, or sweaty? When you have to give a speech or talk to your boss or speak to a large group, do your throat and mouth get exceedingly dry?

Social anxiety has a number of physical manifestations that can be downright humiliating and can make you feel self-conscious. Instead of hiding from your embarrassment, try this merciful meditation for quelling your discomfort and restoring tenderness. Try making an audio recording of this meditation, speaking slowly and pronouncing each word deliberately and with clarity and calmness.

1. *Rest in a comfortable position. Begin to slowly follow your breath.*

2. *Amidst your worst blushing experience and feelings of shame, consider what embarrassment might mean to you.*

3. *You might be shy and awkward at times, but you are also kindhearted, generous, and good-natured to a great many people in your life. Your ability to exhibit embarrassment outwardly signifies that you are a kind and sensitive person.*

Your blush conveys that you are a good listener, you take pride in the work you do, you want to do the best you can, and you care about how others perceive you. You are sympathetic and concerned for others. These are qualities to be admired and respected. Make a mental list of the qualities that you appreciate about yourself, such as being friendly, respectful, courteous, charitable, empathetic, and so on.

4. *Imagine that with each in breath, you're drawing in your strengths and good traits. Let these wonderful qualities permeate your whole body. You feel yourself standing taller and with more confidence to face any circumstance.*

5. *And on each out breath, imagine that you are releasing the awkwardness, shame, and mortified feelings in your body. The redness is passing and vanishing. Your body is finding a peaceful position where you can feel relaxed and at ease no matter what arises. Your beautiful personality and assets outnumber your insecurities. You are more than the sum of your embarrassments.*

When you're ready, end the meditation and walk around, gently moving your body as you carry the benefits of your practice into the world.

12.

surrender pose

Many people experience uncontrollable muscle twitches and spasms as physical symptoms of their anxiety. Some people experience eye twitching. Anxiety leads others to stutter and stammer through conversations, feeling as if their throats were tied in knots. If you feel like your body betrays you when you're anxious, take a breather with these next simple, calming yoga poses. Yoga has been shown to reduce anxiety and stress. These poses offer a unique opportunity to feel centered and grounded and to unify your mind, body, and spirit.

1. *Get into some loose-fitting clothing and remove your shoes.*

2. *Find a peaceful space or room where you won't be interrupted.*

3. *Begin by sitting on the floor with your legs crossed and rest your hands on your knees.*

4. *With your eyes open or closed, focus on your posture, upright but not tense. Breathe in this grounded feeling through your buttocks. Hold this relaxing pose for a few minutes.*

5. *Next, reach your arms upward toward the sky and then slowly return them to your sides. You can raise and lower*

your arms as many times as you desire. Do what feels comfortable. Continue breathing in the calm and breathing out any muscle tension or spasms.

6. *Finally, still seated with your legs crossed, place your hands in the prayer position and hold that position. Chant aloud or inwardly "Om" or try vocalizing your exhalation by saying "Ahh. . . ." Try this for several breaths. Visualize surrendering to a peaceful state of mind, body, and soul.*

For many people, yoga has become a popular practice for getting back into their bodies, lowering their stress, and calming their minds and bodies simultaneously. You can draw on this feeling of calm the next time your body tells you you're feeling anxious.

loving-kindness body scan: developing affection and gratitude for your body

Old, unconscious habits of meanness, self-criticism, and judgment can easily and quickly focus toxic attitudes on your body. For example, how do you usually react to and treat your body when it is sick, hurts, or is injured? Are you angry or kind?

In longer formal sessions and informally for a few breaths at a time, the following meditation—focusing loving-kindness on your body—can help you cultivate a wiser and friendlier relationship with your body in any situation. This practice can be especially helpful in times of anxiety and worry when your "fear body" is looming large.

1. *Take a comfortable position for meditation. It may help to close your eyes.*

2. *Steady yourself and focus attention with mindful breathing for a few minutes.*

3. *Now, shift attention to the flow of all physical sensations through your inner body. Open to and gently notice the direct*

sensations, for example, noticing and feeling the heaviness, the vibration, the heat or coolness, contractions, pulsations, and sensations of expansion or release as they flow and change throughout your body.

4. Recognize this flow of sensations as the flow of life through you in this moment, as the actual feeling of being alive in a living body. If you like, express gratitude to your body for sustaining you in this life. You could speak kindly to your body, saying something like "Thank you, body—may you be happy and well."

5. Shift attention to any part or region of your body that you like, for example, a foot or a finger, a hip or an eyeball, or the expanding chest or the falling belly. Let your focus move to and settle on any body part that calls you or that seems to need closer care and attention.

6. Look more deeply, and open to the sensations in that part. As you feel the sensations, imagine speaking to that part or region with kindness and gratitude, for example, "Thank you for what you do to sustain me in this life. I appreciate you. May you be safe and well."

7. Move your attention around in your body, looking and sensing deeply and offering gratitude and kind wishes. For example, in your chest, include your heart, lungs, and the great blood vessels; in your belly, remember the organs of digestion and their nerves and blood supply; in your pelvis, recall the organs of sex and reproduction and those devoted to eliminating bodily wastes.

8. *You don't have to get too "heady" or even know much about anatomy. Work with what you do know and what you can know. Letting yourself simply feel the sensations of life flowing through each part and region of your body will be good enough.*

9. *Include any part where there is sickness, hurt, or injury. Let your mindful breath go directly in and out of that area as you speak kindly and compassionately to the part involved.*

10. *Practice with any part or as many parts—even your whole body—for as long as you like.*

11. *Finish by opening your eyes and moving gently. Let kindness and appreciation for your body grow.*

stillness within

Chronic anxiety frequently triggers feelings of restlessness or being on edge. You might be someone who is startled easily by the slightest unfamiliar sound or a sudden shift in surroundings. Or maybe you find yourself wringing your hands with nervous energy, unable to sit still and quiet your mind. Don't let this edgy sensation rob you of your right to remain calm and steady through any situation.

1. *Set aside what you're doing. Find a quiet place where you won't be disturbed.*

2. *Sit with your legs crossed on the floor or lie down flat on your back with your arms at your side.*

3. *Take several minutes to pay attention to your breathing. Inhale the calm; exhale the tension. Inhale the quiet; exhale the noise. Inhale the peace; exhale the disquiet.*

4. *You are giving yourself permission to slow down, suspend your racing mind and jittery body, and just sit or lie still.*

5. *Speak your intentions: "I am releasing this nervous energy. I am letting go of this jumpy feeling inside. By being still and quiet, I am reminding my mind and body that stillness and*

tranquility reside within me at all times. I am guiding my mind and body to a place of undisturbed serenity."

6. *In the silence, there is only you and your breath. There is only a timeless continuum of peace and quiet reserved for you whenever you call upon it.*

Let the long-term therapeutic benefits of this exercise calmly surprise you.

support for your adrenals

Prolonged and persistent stress puts excessive strain on your adrenal glands, which are responsible for regulating your stress response. Adrenal exhaustion is a common physical condition that frequently occurs with chronic anxiety, which further taxes your health and aggravates your anxiety. When you keep your body in a constant state of stress, your adrenal glands become exhausted and can underfunction. You may experience low stress tolerance, lethargy, fatigue, light sensitivity, hypoglycemia, and insomnia, to name only a few.

Your adrenals are an important defense against stressful situations. It's time to give your adrenals a rest and commit to a daily practice of relaxation.

1. *From a seated position or lying down, listen to the steady rhythm of your breath. If you are holding your breath or taking short, shallow breaths, this is your opportunity to take slow, deep breaths from your abdomen. Fill your lungs with the oxygen of vibrant life and then empty your lungs of the strenuous drain of stress.*

2. *Speak your intentions: "I am quieting my mind, body, and spirit to allow leisure to flow through easily. I am cutting the ties to my stress and anxiety organ by organ—heart,*

liver, glands, spleen, pancreas, stomach, brain, and so on. I am severing the lines of tension that I store in my head, neck, face, shoulders, arms, hands, chest, belly, back, hips, legs, and feet. My mind has become a sieve, and I am relinquishing my anxious thoughts."

3. *Visualize a calmness infusing every internal organ in your body. You are restoring peace to each overworked part of your body.*

Proper adrenal support must be addressed from a variety of health fronts—diet, supplementation, lifestyle changes, and stress reduction. If you suspect that you have adrenal exhaustion, please consult your holistic physician, naturopath, or other health practitioner for additional consultation for this condition.

fountain of your heart: a visualization for well-being and happiness in yourself and others

Simple visualizations can be powerful forms of meditation. Let your imagination flourish and carry you as you connect with the deep inner feelings of generosity and happiness that can arise in this meditation.

You can practice this meditation in longer formal sessions and informally for just a few breaths at a time. Learn to take this meditation with you. Try it out in many different moments and situations of daily living.

It can help to have someone read the meditation to you, or you can record it and play it back a few times until you make it your own.

1. *Take a comfortable position and close your eyes.*

2. *Place your attention on your breath and breathe mindfully for a few moments.*

3. *When you are ready, shift attention and visualize yourself standing beside a beautiful and amazing fountain in your heart.*

4. *The fountain is in the center of a vast and radiant space and from it flows the clearest and purest water you have ever seen. It is a place of great safety and happiness.*

5. *Let yourself relax and smile.*

6. *Notice that the air temperature is perfect and that the light everywhere is sparkling and bright.*

7. *Beside the fountain are empty cups. Each cup is beautiful and fits comfortably in your hand. Taking one, you fill it from the fountain and drink from it.*

8. *Notice how good the water is. It is the sweetest and freshest water you have ever tasted. It is cool and satisfying. You can feel yourself being refreshed and renewed with each sip. You can feel happiness and contentment filling you.*

9. *Now imagine inviting friends and loved ones into this space to share the fountain of your heart. They enter one at a time. You offer each one a cup of the delicious water. You can see them smiling and relaxing. You can feel their happiness and relief.*

10. *Bring as many others to your fountain as you like. Bring whomever you like. There is plenty of room and plenty of water for everyone. As they drink from the fountain, let their happiness and ease fill you, too.*

11. *Whenever you wish, drink again. Satisfy and fill yourself.*

12. *Rest in the joy and ease that surrounds you.*

13. *May all beings be happy.*

create your own

What places or parts of yourself need your kindness and compassion now? What people in your life need your kindness and compassion?

Use the space below to create your own meditation or practice for cherishing and befriending. Let mindfulness and kindness guide you. Look closely, listen deeply, and trust yourself.

_____

_____

_____

_____

_____

_____

_____

_____

_____

_____

daily meditations for
connecting to the
web of life

Today when I notice uncomfortable feelings based in pain or fear, I will acknowledge those feelings consciously and compassionately and will practice including them in a larger view of interconnectedness.

IN THIS SECTION

Driven by pain, upset, or threat, feelings of fear, isolation, anger, and vulnerability intensify and can temporarily obscure the deeper truths of interrelatedness, affection, and wisdom available in each moment.

Blinded by fear and anxiety, you quickly become lost in "me" and forgetful of "we." Feeling isolated and vulnerable, you are easily manipulated as well, falling victim to those who preach fear and promise relief and safety, regardless of how unrealistic or at what cost.

A much wiser and more compassionate course is available to each human being, in each moment. Sane responses, even in the midst of great anxiety, fear, threat, and despair, can be discerned and accomplished through mindful attention and by knowing how to keep your heart open.

You have been learning about mindfulness, kindness, and compassion throughout this book and experiencing these qualities directly, in different situations and under changing conditions, as you have been doing the meditations. Mindfulness, kindness, and compassion are powerful allies and will not fail you in changing your perception of whatever happens in your life or in supporting a more effective relationship to the people and situations you meet. Compassionate presence can inform your actions and increase your effectiveness in meeting any challenge, including fear, anxiety, and panic.

The practices in this chapter point to another and larger focus for your mindful and compassionate attention. The deliberate shift in view that these meditations offer reveals another approach for you to explore for soothing your worried mind and for remembering your wholeness. By turning your attention to a larger view (deliberately beyond, but inclusive of, "I, me, mine"), you open the possibility for immediate realization of the amazing web of interconnections and interdependencies linking all living things in each moment. By reestablishing yourself in this larger perspective on life, the isolating tendencies of fear and the toxic distortions of anxiety are weakened, and you can more consciously reinhabit your wholeness as a human being.

A larger view recognizes the experiences of pain (physical or emotional, including fear, despair, and anxiety) and isolation and includes those challenges in a wise understanding of the role and function of such upset in the long trajectory of your own life. A larger view also sees and appreciates commonality—in good times and bad—with other human beings and indeed all other life forms. Seeing that the places and situations that seem uniquely personal actually also exist in the felt experience of others, you sense more directly the links and connections in the web of life.

The meditations and practices in this section focus on both of these aspects of taking the larger view of yourself embedded within the web of all life. Some practices and meditations in this section point toward seeking greater insight into your encounters with personal challenges, while others point toward finding a deeper appreciation for your connections and place in the family of things.

By turning toward the present moment mindfully and with mercy, and radically accepting whatever is happening, you can change the reactive habits of isolation and separation as they arise in heart, mind, and body. Learning to trust yourself and mindfulness, and investigating the larger view and network of interconnections, can be profoundly helpful in freeing yourself from the reactive habits of isolation and separation generated by fear and anxiety.

AS YOU PRACTICE

Exploring these meditations and practices, remember the following statements and see what truth lies there for you.

- *Everything you see, feel, and think is changing.* By dwelling mindfully in the present moment, you gain the ability to see the truth of change and impermanence in everything within and around you. What will you need to be able to relate most wisely to this truth of change?

- *Beware of taking yourself (and your thoughts or beliefs) too seriously.* Thoughts and beliefs, including negative judgments about yourself and others, are also subject to change and are often based on incorrect or incomplete information. Paying close attention with an open mind and an open heart can help keep you from the prison of erroneous rigidity! Laughing at yourself frequently can too.

- *Look deeply. What is here now contains the elements and momentum of the past.* A wooden chair is only one stage in the life of a tree. A raisin contains the nutrients and energy it took to grow the grape. The chair and the raisin cannot be here without the other elements. What does this reflection mean for your "larger view" of what it means to be "you"? What does it say about your place in the family of things?

- *What happens now shapes the future.* Just as the elements of the past live here in the present, so too what happens now carries over into the next moment and the next and so on. How might this connection between present and future moments relate to your experience and reactions to fear, anxiety, or other distress? What might this connection mean for your relationships with others and in the world?

keep in mind

- Feeling separated from parts of yourself and painfully distant from others in your life happens easily. But such feelings actually belie deeper truths of wholeness and interrelatedness.

- Learning to hold both fear reactions and feelings of isolation with mercy while taking a larger and longer view of experiences unfolding in the present moment offers you another approach to freeing your anxious mind.

- By consciously reinhabiting your place in the web of life, you can soothe and calm your fears and worries and recover a sense of balance and the felt experience of connection with others.

in this moment: reentering the flow of life

This practice may be done as a thoughtful reflection or as a loving-kindness meditation for yourself or another.

Use any or all of the phrases and verses that resonate for you. Use them in any order that makes sense. It could be helpful to do mindful breathing between verses or even between phrases.

In this moment—
> *Feeling assaulted and vulnerable to*
> *Intimidation, danger, suffering, and injustice in this world,*
I breathe consciously,
> *Knowing life can be fierce and mysterious, I look closer.*
> *May I find the means to cease hating, to open my heart,*
> *and to act wisely.*

In this moment—
> *Recognizing my previous dependence upon outer sources for*
> *Happiness, security, and certainty,*
I breathe consciously,
> *Knowing that all these sources are subject to change, I grow*
> *wiser.*

> *May I recognize and cherish all of my supports while they are here, and*
> *Release them freely when they must leave me or I must leave them.*

In this moment—
> *Growing intimacy with my inner life reveals extremes of*
> *Fear and arrogance, vulnerability and egotism, confusion and certainty,*
> *Hatred and enchantment.*

I breathe consciously,
> *Knowing my wholeness is greater than any of these conditions, I gain release from their spell.*
> *May I stay present and not lose sight of my true relationship with all living things.*

In all the moments and breaths I am given—including the last one,
> *May I grow in awareness, wisdom, and compassion.*
> *May these reflections awaken in me*
> *Wonder, trust, gratitude, and affection for the blessings of this life.*

prayer scroll

Some Japanese Buddhists pray by chanting and sitting on the floor before a *gohonzon*, an object of worship or a prayer scroll displayed inside a box with doors on it. Whether you follow an organized religion or not, the therapeutic benefits of prayer have been demonstrated in many health studies. The following exercise is an occasion to create your own personalized prayer scroll and to inspire you to bring daily ritual and prayer into your life.

Prayer can take countless forms—chanting, singing, repeating mantras or affirmations, or quiet solitude. You may pray before each meal as a way of saying grace and giving gratitude. The act of praying can be a personal and private communication with your higher spirit or creator.

1. *You'll need a piece of paper and pen. You might prefer nice stationery or colorful wrapping paper.*

2. *Begin by writing out your own daily prayer for yourself (for example, "May I be free from harm. May I be loved and give love. May I be safe. May I be happy and well. May I be healthy"). Say aloud or silently the prayer that you've created.*

3. *Now write down a daily prayer for your loved ones (for example, "May they be free from harm. May they be loved and give love. May they be safe. May they be happy and well. May they be healthy"). Say aloud or silently these prayers for others.*

4. *Finally, write out a daily prayer for all living beings and the planet (for example, "May there be peace on earth. May there be health and harmony. May there be loving-kindness for all"). Say aloud or silently these prayers to the universe.*

5. *Feel free to repeat these positive affirmations several times, speaking your sincere intentions into each word over and over again.*

3.

affirming forgiveness

Accumulated stress and anxiety can lead you to blame, find fault, or point the finger at others. You may have old wounds inflicted by someone else. You may consider that person to be your worst enemy. You may hold resentment toward your parents, ex-partner, best friend, or boss. Maybe someone betrayed you, and you still hate that person for it.

Resentment is venomous and can surge through your mind and body, wreaking havoc and alarm. This forgiveness meditation will steer you in the direction of deeper healing and personal resolution.

1. *Bring to mind a person who has caused you harm or brought sorrow to your life. If it is painful to think of her face, then substitute a name or item to symbolize her.*

2. *Be aware of the feelings that are stirring inside you. Maybe you feel outrage, sadness, hopelessness, or paranoia at the thought of running into her.*

3. *Be mindful of the sensations that are bubbling up inside you. You may feel that you are burning with bitterness, tingling with fear, or close to tears.*

4. *Say aloud the following affirmation: "I wish this person only love, beauty, truth, and joy." Repeat ten times, saying it slowly with sincerity and loving-kindness.*

5. *Now imagine the darkness lifting from the space around you. You can feel a calm, cooling sensation starting on your face and spreading outward across your whole body. It will become more difficult to cling to hatred and you will begin to feel a lightness in your heart, a weightlessness in your whole being. There is only compassion beaming out from every pore in your body. There is only forgiveness.*

This may take practice. If you find it to be too challenging offering forgiveness to someone who's done you great harm, begin by offering forgiveness to someone you love who did something almost inconsequential—like your partner for not doing the dishes. Practicing on someone you care about can help prime your pump for those who pose a greater challenge to your ability to forgive.

the web of support: a reflection and thanksgiving before eating

Taking a larger view includes a conscious consideration of the sources of support and nurturance in your life. Looking more deeply, you can see the amazing web of interrelatedness and interdependency that supports us all.

Pausing before any meal to reflect and give thanks is widely practiced. The following reflection and thanksgiving can be done regardless of your particular faith or religious tradition.

Let deepening awareness of blessings and supports, and consciousness of your natural interrelatedness to others, calm and soothe any fears or anxiety you are carrying.

1. *Before beginning to eat, pause, breathe mindfully, and notice your food.*

2. *Looking at the food, consider the following, even saying it quietly if you like.*

   Earth, water, fire, wind, space
   Countless others gave their lives and energy that I might eat—
   —in these circumstances, in this moment.
   May their gifts be recognized and appreciated.
   May their generosity and gifts benefit all living things.

Here are some thoughts for further reflection:

- *Earth, water, fire, wind, space.* Consider the elemental nature of life and your own life. How are these elements requirements for living? Where do you find them? What sustains them? What help and support do the elements need?

- *Countless others gave their lives and energy that I might eat.* Looking deeply, can you see the origins of your food? What did it take to produce it? Who had to sacrifice for you to have it before you? Who died and who lived in the process?

- *In these circumstances, in this moment.* Look around you. Where are you? How did that come to pass? How did you obtain or pay for your food? What had to happen for you to be able to do that? Over your lifetime, what and who helped you be able to be here now, in these circumstances?

- *May their gifts be recognized and appreciated.* As you look deeply and reflect, the gifts may appear to be endless. Let this recognition awaken a deeper sense of gratitude in you. Let it deepen your appreciation for the web of life.

- *May their gifts benefit all living things.* What will you do with your precious life and talents? How are you passing on the blessings of those whose gifts enabled you to eat? Reflect on your actual capacity to impact and benefit the world and on your requirements for nutrition and support in order to realize that capacity.

new glasses

New possibilities arise when you change your perspective. It's similar to putting on a new pair of glasses and seeing an old problem with "new" eyes. Sometimes the simple act of shifting your focus can give you a better outlook on your situation.

Let's say that you're having a nerve-racking morning or a frustrating workday. You might try to shift your focus toward something that brings you joy, makes you laugh, or reminds you how loved you are, such as a rosebush blooming in your yard or a favorite photograph or a homemade gift from your children.

Changing your outlook on stress can literally mean focusing away from the source of tension and refocusing on something calming and pleasurable.

1. *When stressful thoughts threaten to ruin your day, close your eyes for a moment and pretend you're putting on your rose-colored glasses. These glasses allow you to see the lighter side of life. They remind you that everything is okay, it'll work itself out, and everyone is going to be fine. Your new glasses clarify your vision and bring to light the beauty that surrounds you. They allow you to see the precious moments that often slip past you without much notice, such as the good-bye*

kiss from your partner or the starburst smile from your child
or the friendly wave of greeting from your neighbor.

2. *What does the world look like through your new glasses?*

6.

sea of tranquility

No matter how much control you may think you have, life is unpredictable. People, places, and things change, sometimes gradually and other times rapidly. Just as you start to feel secure with one way of doing things, life changes course, and you're faced with growing uncertainty. There may be no realistic, foolproof way to be fully prepared for change, but there is a way to keep your perspective.

There are limitless meditations that can guide you through change and ambiguity. Here is one of them. Try making an audio recording of this meditation, speaking slowly, and deliberately pronouncing each word with clarity and calmness.

1. *Close your eyes and visualize yourself at the beach, sitting on the warm sands, with a refreshing sea breeze sprinkling your whole body. You are safe and secure. You are watching the waves drift in and out, over and over again. Each wave is like your breath, rising up inside from deep within and then releasing and returning out to sea.*

2. *What do you notice about the surface of the ocean? It's much like your life—some parts are rough, choppy, with impending waves of uncertainty pounding away. Breathe in these moments that are challenging and upsetting. Remember that*

you have the stability and strength to weather the storm. Breathe out your fears and doubts about the outcome. What will be will be. Only the waves can carry all your secrets and anxieties out to sea.

3. *What's happening below the surface of the ocean? It is a calm, serene, quiet, and contemplative underwater experience. Schools of fish are swimming to-and-fro. Sea plants are sashaying to a mysterious, musical current. Starfish cling to rocks in colorful display. Luminescent shards of sunlight splice through the water, transmitting warmth and radiance downward.*

4. *Depending on what life tosses your way, you may be body-surfing the big one or floating along a sea of serenity. Be mindful of the journey, the highs and lows, the good times and the bad, the joy and the pain. Move gently with each wave.*

When you're ready, bring your attention back to the room around you. Carry the calm tide of the ocean within you as you move through your day.

what are you asking me? a conversation with your fear

Avoidance of the fear-evoking object or situation is said to be one of the maintaining factors of chronic anxiety. What if, rather than moving away from the fear, you turned toward it, consciously?

Viktor Frankl survived Auschwitz in large measure by learning to appreciate and articulate the importance of finding meaning in challenging situations (Frankl 1959). He believed that human beings must respond to and find meaning for themselves in the challenges of each life if they are to live fully and wholly. Another way to put Frankl's insight is to ask yourself: "What is life asking me in this situation?"

Use this meditation to have a conversation with your fears and worries and see if they have anything important to tell you about living.

1. *Take a comfortable position.*

2. *Collect and steady yourself by breathing mindfully for a few minutes.*

3. *When you feel ready, open your focus and deliberately recall a situation or relationship that evokes anxious or fearful*

thoughts in you. Welcome the entire experience and gently and kindly make room for whatever arises.

4. *Breathe mindfully at times for a few breaths when you need to anchor yourself in the presence of the fear and anxiety.*

5. *Now imagine speaking directly to the fear or anxiety as if it were a person having tea with you. Speak as if you were seeking its advice, even though the fear or anxiety is intimidating or unsettling for you.*

6. *Remember to breathe mindfully when you need to.*

7. *Ask the fear or anxiety what it needs or what it is trying to tell you. Pause and listen deeply with an open heart and an open mind for all answers.*

8. *Ask any other questions you need to for clarity. Respect all responses, knowing they are only information to be used for your health and well-being.*

9. *Finish by offering thank-yous to the fear and anxiety, and to yourself for your courage.*

10. *What have you learned?*

the gift of anxiety

How can your worst fear possibly be a gift, you may ask. All your life you've beaten yourself up for having anxiety. You drive your kids crazy with your constant cautionary advice. Your friends don't understand. It has adversely affected your relationships, job, and even your free time or vacation. And there doesn't seem to be a cure on the horizon.

"Show me the evidence that something good has come out of being an incessant worrier racked with anxiety," you demand. You most certainly can't see the positive if you're stuck with a long list of negatives.

Let's take this time to highlight the pearls of wisdom that often get ignored at the height of your fear and doubt. Make a mental or written list of a few potentially positive aspects of living with anxiety, such as the following:

- My anxiety is a gift that permits me to be cautious and not take unnecessary risks that could bring harm to others or myself.

- My anxiety is a gift that gives me greater understanding and empathy for others who also live with it.

- My anxiety is a gift that allows me to experience a wide array of emotions and feelings. I am emotionally expressive and full of feelings.

- My anxiety is a gift that I have harnessed and channeled successfully into creative outlets, such as yoga and writing.

- My anxiety is a gift that has given me the ability to be more sensitive to others and myself.

- My anxiety is a gift that _____ (*fill in for yourself*).

Your positive personality traits are reminders to believe in yourself, even when self-doubt or negative self-talk tries to deprive you of your strengths and beauty.

transformational tales

Charles Dickens' classic tale *A Christmas Carol* tells the story of Ebenezer Scrooge, who is visited by ghosts that allow him to finally see things from a different perspective, which radically transforms him in the end. Each ghost delivers insight into Scrooge's past, present, and future behavior. It also changes how he treats others. Because of these unique visions, he is able to witness firsthand his cruel actions and the consequences of his cruelty, and then change his ways.

What spirits might visit you, and what would they reveal? This next exercise will help you identify unhelpful or negative patterns and change your behavior in order to foster personal transformation.

1. *Consider what spirit of the past might pay you a visit. Maybe you can recall a particularly unpleasant memory of a lost friendship or a breakup or a time when things turned out for the worst. Although you can't change the past, what can you learn from those experiences? Maybe you need to brush up on your communication skills in order to prevent frequent misunderstandings or conflicts.*

2. *What's happening with you in this present moment? Maybe you're restless and fretting about a project that you're working*

on. Maybe you're stressed about studying for an upcoming exam. Maybe you're bothered by a confusing e-mail from your friend and are concerned about a miscommunication. What can your present conflicts tell you about how you handle stress and ways you might improve? Do you need to exercise? Have you done anything nice for yourself today? Is there something you're procrastinating on? If so, take action in the present to live a life free of anxiety.

3. *Take a brief minute to reflect on your future. Do you see yourself being happy? Do you believe you will be fulfilled? What action can you take now to help you move toward a future that brings you joy?*

Reflections into your past, present, and future are windows of opportunities for making changes, asking for help, finding a new path, and opening new doorways for transformation. When you confront your ghosts, you can kick-start your motivation to put your best foot forward in different ways, starting right now.

the end of resentment: a forgiveness meditation

Forgiveness can be thought of as the end of resentment. When resentment is carried around, untended, it can be the trigger or the maintaining cause for anxiety about encounters with another, or it can influence how you talk to and blame yourself for a wide variety of things. Withheld and denied feelings of anger and hurt fuel resentment. Practicing forgiveness can release these feelings and remove the nourishment they provide to resentment and the feelings of separation and isolation resentment creates.

Whenever you recognize that your inner and outer worlds are contracted and enmeshed in patterns of resentment, try the following forgiveness meditation. As you practice, you will probably find that this meditation works in both formal and informal situations and can be a powerful ally in even the harshest moments. Also, as you practice, remember to include self-forgiveness in your meditation.

In these practices, forgiveness is *offered* because we have no control over other people or their feelings. The best we can do is to offer and ask for forgiveness. The language also acknowledges that hurt can arise from both intentional and unintentional actions.

As you practice each of these aspects of forgiveness, breathe mindfully and remain open to all responses arising in you, meeting them with acceptance and compassion.

1. Offering forgiveness when someone hurts you. *Think of someone who has hurt you in some way. Imagine speaking kindly to them. Say something like, "For any hurt you may have caused me, intentional or unintentional, I offer forgiveness."*

2. Asking forgiveness of someone you have hurt. *Think of someone you may have hurt in some way. Imagine speaking kindly to them. Say something like, "For any hurt I may have caused you, intentional or unintentional, I ask your forgiveness."*

3. Offering yourself forgiveness for any hurt you may have caused. *Think of yourself in a situation of being hurt or of causing hurt. Imagine speaking kindly to yourself in either situation. Say something like, "For any hurt I may have caused in this situation, intentional or unintentional, I offer myself forgiveness."*

stop the spin cycle

There are times when your mind gets stuck in an endless loop of problems and possible worrisome outcomes with no end in sight. This is most agonizing at night when it prevents you from getting a good night's rest. This next meditation will help you disengage from the spin cycle.

Before you start this exercise, get comfy in your bed, tucked in, and relax your body. This will alert your overactive brain that you mean business; it's time to shut down and usher in dreamtime. This exercise can also be done while kneeling at your bedside each night with the lights out, as if to pray. Consider making an audio recording of this meditation, speaking slowly and pronouncing each word deliberately and with clarity and calmness.

Sleep awaits you, but first your mind wants to play games and remind you who's in charge. It may want to run a few laps around the mental court in case it has forgotten any last details.

Take your mind on a journey to the ends of the universe. This journey begins with giving thanks, starting at the microscopic level and eventually branching out to the macroscopic.

1. Let's start with you: *I am grateful for this body of cells, molecules, blood, veins, arteries, nerves, organs, muscles,*

tendons, flesh, and bones. I am grateful for my head, face, hair, neck, arms, shoulders, fingers, chest, breasts, back, torso, hips, buttocks, pelvis, thighs, calves, ankles, feet, and toes.

2. Move outward to your surroundings: *I am grateful for this bed, pillow, blankets, comforter, nightstand, lamp, rug, painting, photographs, shoes, clothes, jackets, bedroom, desk, hallway, kitchen, bathroom, living room, dinner table, and home.*

3. Advance further outside your house: *I am grateful for the backyard, front yard, sidewalk, neighbors, cars, café, corner store, laundromat, street, highway, and city. I am grateful for every seed, root, flower, blade of grass, shrub, tree, lawn, and garden. I am grateful for every town, state, country, continent, and the planet Earth. I am grateful for the sky, sun, moon, stars, planets, solar system, universe, and galaxies far and wide. I am grateful for and humbled by our interconnectedness, one and all. I am surrendering my mind, body, and spirit to the free fall of sleep.*

12.

cultivate curiosity

If you live with any kind of fear or insecurity about new things, your ability to develop a sense of wonder can become stagnant. Fostering a willingness to experience something new and different has its own personal rewards and fulfillment. When you nurture your curiosity, you delve deeper into the fullness of life. And in turn, you learn more about yourself and the world in the process.

Next time you find yourself resisting a new hobby or ordering the same-old, same-old or turning down more information about a new subject, try this practice to increase your engagement with the unknown. You might just find more satisfaction and meaning in life.

1. *Cultivating your curiosity begins when you realize your full potential for curiosity. Consider which activities or hobbies you already find pleasure participating in, such as working out at the gym, reading, cooking, quilting, bird-watching, gardening, doing crossword puzzles, biking, hiking, and so on. You might also be an enthusiast in specific subjects, such as plants, computers, psychology, biology, history, and so on.*

2. *What new activity or interest would you be willing to look into or sign up for? You might have an interest in trying a*

different route home from work. You might have longed to visit a foreign country. You might have had a fascination with learning piano as a child but lost interest or got too busy to pursue it as an adult. Consider signing up for a drawing class, joining a book club, or learning swing dancing. For extra support, invite a friend to join you in venturing into a new area of interest that may feel intimidating or frightening.

It's not important to master this new pursuit. Curiosity takes root when you open that book and study more about a certain topic of interest. Finding wonder and inspiration in new things works as a reinforcing counterweight to anxiety and fear. When you exercise your curiosity through new ventures, you don't erase doubt, but it may open you to the positive outcomes and a fresh, innovative outlook on life.

happy together: a meditation on sympathetic joy

Could the joy of another be felt and awaken joy inside of you? Of course! Connected through the web of life, we human beings experience such moments frequently. But how often does another's good fortune awaken different feelings in you?

What if you discovered that by explicitly taking joy in the joy of another (*sympathetic joy*), you could weaken and escape from negative feelings of envy and self-criticism that so often arise, unintended, as reactions to someone else's happiness?

The following is a way, both as formal meditation and informally, to cultivate sympathetic joy. You may be pleased to discover also that sympathetic joy offers you the possibility of relief from maintaining causes of chronic anxiety and worry such as self-criticism and perceived insecurity. How does this work? It is simply that the more happiness you can feel and sustain through interconnectedness with others, the less power the fear and isolation will have over you. Here's sympathetic joy as a formal meditation:

1. *Take a comfortable position and breathe mindfully for a few minutes.*

2. *Think of a friend or loved one who recently experienced good fortune.*

3. *Picture them. Let yourself smile and relax as you recall their happiness.*

4. *Reflect on their good fortune and how they benefited. Let yourself open to the joy and ease they feel. Notice any joy or a smile that comes to you as you reflect.*

5. *Imagine speaking to them with affection and gratitude. You might say something like, "May your good fortune never end!" or "May you always be so happy!"*

6. *Allow yourself to bathe in the feelings of happiness and ease that arise.*

7. *Practice as long as you like, immersed and at rest in feelings of joy and well-being.*

Here's sympathetic joy practiced informally in daily life:

1. *When someone shares their good news or good fortune with you, either immediately with them or privately with yourself, later on, practice responding with enthusiasm and a statement such as "May your good fortune and happiness never end!" or "May you always be so happy!"*

2. *Before saying anything, deliberately turn toward the other person's feelings of joy and well-being and let those feelings awaken the same feelings in you. Rest in those feelings after*

you speak and later as you recall and reflect on the other person.

3. *Let the feelings of happiness and well-being arising in you sustain and comfort you.*

When your mind wanders or other thoughts appear while doing either of these forms of practice, know that you have *not* made a mistake. Just let those thoughts go and return your attention to the feelings of joy. Remember that thoughts are just thoughts. You don't have to fight them or feed them. This meditation is about experiencing and enjoying feelings of happiness.

healing time

If you suffer from chronic pain or illness combined with anxiety, you may feel depleted by a feeling of hopelessness. The following is a guided meditation for making time for healing and recovery for yourself and others. Make an audio recording of your healing meditation, speaking slowly, and deliberately pronouncing each word with clarity and calmness. Try to listen to the entire recording in a relaxed state of mind, once a day. With continued practice, this meditation will help you let go of the battle with your pain or illness and unlock the gateways to healing.

1. *The time for healing is now. You are letting your body relax and get the rest that it desperately needs. There is no need to hurry or work through any problems right now. Let go of your work schedule, to-do list, e-mails, phone calls, and errands. Detach from all your distractions and activities. Your body has a natural rhythm, and you are escorting your body to a place of rest and relaxation. Resist any urges to break this flow of silent stillness for some pressing item that you just remembered. It can wait. You can wait.*

2. *Be patient with your body in the resting state so you can resurface with renewed health, vitality, and strength. In this*

restful space, you are letting go of anger, fear, and stressful thoughts. There's no room for them here. There's no need to struggle against your condition. Struggling doesn't serve you, and it rarely improves your situation.

3. *It has been a difficult and frustrating path to feel pain or to carry illness for such a long time. That is why this healing meditation is so necessary. When your body and spirit get to relax, the real healing begins.*

4. *Now imagine a healing beam of light encircling your body, radiating good health and well-being. Visualize this radiant healing energy pulsating outward as it encircles your friends, family, and loved ones. Gradually let this healing force manifest across every human, every living species, and our planet—restoring health, vigor, and harmony to one and all.*

15.

love without limits

For a great many, the power of love is indisputable. We're not talking about romantic love or even friendship love. Unconditional love involves the absolute willingness to care for the welfare of another without conditions, judgment, or guidelines. This means that you love without strings attached, regardless of how a person acts or behaves. You let go of the past. You offer compassion and understanding without expectation or desire for something in return. Unconditional love swells when you are giving more love to others as well as receiving more of it in your life.

So how can you increase your capacity to give and receive unconditional love? Take this moment to open your heart to loved ones, community, nature, and the cosmos with a breathing incantation. Find a meditative space, sit quietly, close your eyes, take a deep breath in, and then silently repeat each phrase in combination with each out breath. Try this for several minutes.

The spirit of love is all around me.
I embody the spirit of love.
Love resides in me and others at all times.
I am moving in the direction of love.
Others are moving in the direction of love.
I am letting go of fear, which pushes others away.
I am embracing love, which draws others near.
Love allows me to feel connected and cherished.
When I love, I allow others to feel connected and cherished.
Grant me the strength to give love without limits.
Grant me the strength to receive love without limits.
The human heart has the capacity to love all people, places,
     and things at all times.
Love is a force of nature that cannot be stopped.
Love is a gift from the soul to be shared with the universe.
Love is abundant, and there is enough love for everyone.

16.

prepare yourself to follow me: a meditation on death and wisdom

All living things connected within the web of life are also connected by the reality of death.

The end of these physical bodies is inevitable, yet how often does denial or fearful imagination about the reality of death distort and shadow how we live and relate to others in each moment?

In the unwillingness to acknowledge change and death as part of life, and in the unexplored fears surrounding grief and feelings of vulnerability, lie dangerous seeds for maintaining anxiety and worry about a wide range of life experience and situations.

So in the interest of calming your anxious mind, we offer this meditation on the truth of death and the wisdom that awaits anyone who opens to that truth. Through wise and compassionate acknowledging of the naturalness of death, and a meditative reflection on deep fears about change, vulnerability, and loss of control, you may empower yourself to open to and experience an awakening to life, in all of its mystery, that can astound you.

There are many ways to reflect and to meditate on death and mortality. The following is one example. You may wish to seek and practice others, as well. Let them all inform you.

1. *Give yourself plenty of time as well as a peaceful place for this practice.*

2. *Take a comfortable position, even lying down, if you like.*

3. *Breathe mindfully for a few minutes, settling into the present moment.*

4. *It can help as you relax and enter this meditation to visualize yourself surrounded and protected by a luminous ball of beautiful light. Or, if you prefer, imagine that you are being held in the arms of, or resting in the lap of, the highest and most sacred being you can imagine.*

5. *When you feel ready, begin to reflect as follows.*

6. *Speak slowly and quietly to yourself the following phrases, noting and allowing all of your responses. You may wish to pause between the phrases and breathe mindfully.*

   - *"No one is exempt from death."*
   - *"Death can come at any time and in many ways."*
   - *"Neither wealth nor the love or efforts of others can keep us from death."*

7. *After speaking and listening to your responses, ask yourself this:*

    - *"How could I better and more deeply accept and act on the truth of death?"*

    - *"Does my fear or resistance to this truth interfere with my life? How?"*

    - *"How might I relate more wisely and compassionately to myself and others if I embraced the reality of death, loss, and vulnerability more consciously?"*

Continue your meditation and reflections as long as you wish. Practice them as often as you find helpful. Let the wisdom you gain give you courage, joy, and appreciation for the preciousness of your life and all of your relations.

17.

create your own

What challenges or blessings are happening in your life now that remind or point you to something greater and larger?

Use the space below to create your own meditation or practice for taking the larger view and realizing your place in the family of things. Let mindfulness and kindness guide you. Look closely, listen deeply, and trust yourself.

_____

_____

_____

_____

_____

_____

_____

_____

_____

_____

_____

_____

_____

_____

_____

_____

epilogue

We live in the present moment.

We also live in these physical forms and share our lives with other human beings and an amazing array of other living creatures.

And all of us interact and interplay with elemental energies and forces of nature that are constantly shaping and changing our planet, the Earth.

In each moment, to one who looks deeply and opens softly enough, the interconnections and interdependencies of these diverse life forms and life streams are visible. Conditions, actions, consequences, and possibilities become more obvious to the one who can see clearly. Wise and compassionate action follows naturally from conscious presence and clear seeing.

When fear, anxiety, and worry are allowed to distort and drive perceptions and actions, then our possibilities—individually and collectively as a species and for our planet—are limited, and the choices we make too often perpetuate pain and suffering. Locked in the prison of demoralization, helplessness, and despair that follow overwhelming fear and anxiety, the miracle of being human, with its wonderful and awesome possibility, is lost.

Yet each human being already has all they need to escape the limitations and restrictions of fear and anxiety.

By learning the language and skills of awareness, courageously embracing the practice of mindfulness and openhearted attention, and trusting your ability to act on the wisdom that follows from sensitive and kind attention in all moments of life, you become free of the power of fear and anxiety to rule your life. You also become a more effective agent for positive change and healing in our world.

The meditations and practices offered in this book are vehicles and technologies to help you discover the depth and reality of your innate capacity for ease, presence, kindness, and connection in this life. These meditations do not *give* you anything. They simply point you toward what you already are. You only have to go there.

The potential for a radical transformation in personal views and relationships awaits for anyone who makes even one of these practices their own and brings it forward consistently in their life.

By opening—through skills of awareness and kindness—to your wholeness and possibility, you offer new hope to others and to the world.

May you, your loved ones, and all the life in this world benefit from your practice and the resulting gifts of presence and compassion.

references

Begley, S. 2007. *Train Your Mind, Change Your Brain.* New York: Ballantine Books.

Bourne, E. 2005. *The Anxiety and Phobia Workbook.* 4th ed. Oakland, CA: New Harbinger Publications.

Brantley, J. 2007. *Calming Your Anxious Mind: How Mindfulness and Compassion Can Free You from Anxiety, Fear, and Panic.* 2nd ed. (1st ed. 2003). Oakland, CA: New Harbinger Publications.

Frankl, V. 1959. *Man's Search for Meaning.* New York: Pocket Books.

Goleman, D. 2003. *Destructive Emotions.* New York: Bantam Books.

Kabat-Zinn, J. 2005. *Coming to Our Senses: Healing Ourselves and the World Through Mindfulness.* New York: Hyperion.

Kabat-Zinn, J. 2005. *Full Catastrophe Living.* New York: Delta.

Siegel, D. J. 2007. *The Mindful Brain.* New York: Norton.

ADDITIONAL READING

Rosenberg, L., with D. Guy. 2000. *Living in the Light of Death: On the Art of Being Truly Alive.* Boston and London: Shambhala.

Salzberg, S. 2005. *The Force of Kindness.* Boulder, CO: Sounds True, Inc.

Tolle, E. 2005. *A New Earth: Awakening to Your Life's Purpose.* New York: Dutton.

Jeffrey Brantley, MD, is a consulting associate in the Duke Department of Psychiatry and the founder and director of the Mindfulness-Based Stress Reduction Program at Duke University's Center for Integrative Medicine. He is author of *Calming Your Anxious Mind* and coauthor of *Five Good Minutes, Five Good Minutes in the Evening, Five Good Minutes at Work,* and *The Dialectical Behavior Therapy Skills Workbook.*

Wendy Millstine, NC, is a freelance writer and certified holistic nutrition consultant who specializes in diet and stress reduction. She is coauthor of *Five Good Minutes, Five Good Minutes in the Evening,* and *Five Good Minutes at Work.* Millstine lives and works in Oakland, CA.

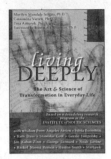